The Myth
of the Jewish Race

The Myth
of the Jewish Race

A Biologist's Point of View

Alain F. Corcos

Lehigh
University
Press

Bethlehem: Lehigh University Press

Associated University Presses
2010 Eastpark Boulevard
Cranbury, NJ 08512

The paper used in this publication meets the requirements of the American National Standard for Permanence of Paper for Printed Library Materials Z39.48-1984.

Library of Congress Cataloging-in-Publication Data

Corcos, Alain F., 1925–
    The myth of the Jewish race : a biologist's point of view / Alain F. Corcos.
        p.   cm.
    Includes bibliographical references and index.
    ISBN 0-934223-79-3 (alk. paper)
        1. Jews—Identity.   2. Race—Social aspects.   3. Human genetics—
    Religious aspects.   I. Title.
    DS143.C675   2005
    305.892′4—dc22   2004024723

PRINTED IN THE UNITED STATES OF AMERICA

This Book Is Dedicated to My Parents
Maurice and Simone Corcos

Contents

Preface

I write to seek understanding . . .
—John Howard Griffin

I CAME TO WRITE THIS BOOK FOR PERSONAL AND SCIENTIFIC REASONS. I was born in France where I spent most of my youth. I was fourteen years old when World War II broke out, and less than a year later France capitulated. My parents, my brother, and I lived first under the fascist Vichy regime and then under the Italian–German occupation. In March 1944, my brother and I escaped from occupied France through Spain and joined the Allied Forces in North Africa. Months later we were sent to the United States for training as air force flying personnel, an odyssey described in my book, *The Little Yellow Train*.[1]

The Vichy government was not only fascist but also the most virulently anti-Semitic regime that ever ruled France. In its efforts to "cleanse the Jewish dirt" from French society, Vichy devised a broader definition of a Jew than that of the German Nazis. According to the latter, a Jew was one who currently or formerly practiced the Jewish religion or a person who had more than two Jewish grandparents. A person with two Jewish grandparents, not affiliated with the Jewish religious community, and not married to a Jew was classified as a non-Jew.

In contrast, Vichy classified a person with two Jewish grandparents as Jewish, which meant that children of a Jew and non-Jew could face deportation to a death camp.[2] This definition applied to my family because some of my ancestors had practiced the Jewish faith. Even though we were not part of the Jewish community, according to Vichy we were Jews. Soon after its establishment Vichy required all persons who fit the definition to register as Jews. My parents' wisdom and courage in refusing to register undoubtedly saved us from death.

9

My whole life has been marked by the fact that I was discriminated against when I was a teenager. I felt deeply, of course, that any type of persecution for any reason was criminal, but in my case the reason was the beliefs held by some of my ancestors. This made no sense at all to me, because I could in no way be responsible for their convictions.

Early in life I discovered that anti-Semites are not concerned about my personal beliefs or even religious doctrines. Rather, they regard Jewishness as inherited, just like original sin, and whereas baptism symbolically cleanses original sin, there is no cleansing for Jewishness. I also discovered that anti-Semites considered Jews to have distinct, inferior, and evil biological characteristics. This concept is based on two false biological premises: that pure races of human beings exist, and that some of these races are superior to others. As a trained biologist and geneticist, I am convinced there are not and never were human races, because groups of people have never been isolated from one another long enough to form distinct races. This conclusion has been reached by an increasing number of anthropologists and biologists over the last fifteen years,[3] and I wrote a book on the subject.[4]

In this book the term *race* is used in its strictly biological sense: a variety or subspecies of mankind. A race arises when a group of people is separated geographically and sexually from other groups for long enough and under sufficient conditions to retain and/or develop an assortment of traits which completely distinguish its members from those of other human groups and which are transmissible by descent.

A friend asked me why I wanted to write a book on the biological myth of the Jewish race when I had just written one on the myth of human races. "If there are no human races," he said, "obviously there is no Jewish race." This is perfectly true, but there is a very important reason. More than fifty years after the death of Hitler, the defeat of Nazism, and the horrors of the Holocaust, the concept of a Jewish race is still alive and well in the minds of too many Jews and non-Jews. There is also a personal reason. I felt this was the only way for me to deal with the persecution that affected my childhood and which I could not forget. My mind is now at peace.

Although many volumes have been written that condemn anti-

Semitism and deal with its history, to my knowledge only two treat the myth of the Jewish race.[5] Oddly, though both maintain that there is no such thing as a Jewish race, the authors write about Jewish blood and Jewish genes, which are misleading concepts as harmful and pernicious as the term *race* itself. In this book I do my best to destroy the false biological premises that undergird the myth of the Jewish race.

Acknowledgments

I WISH TO THANK THE LATE FLOYD MONAGHAN AND JACOB CLIMO FOR their patience in reading parts of the manuscript; and Manfred and Pat Engelmann, Albert Rabin, Leroy and Connie Kesler, and Art Vener for reading the work in its entirety. I am very grateful to Robert Root-Bernstein and Evelyn Rivera for their helpful criticisms which made the book more scholarly and more readable. They also kept me on track when I diverged from the main subject of the book. I owe a debt of gratitude to Elizabeth Johnston who has been an editor extra-ordinaire and to Judy Mayer of Lehigh University Press for her editing skill. Finally, I want to thank my wife, Joanne, for her patience in listening to my outbursts against racism.

Introduction

Strictly speaking, a person is a Jew by virtue of his adherence
to the Jewish religion. If he is not a member of some orga-
nized form of Judaism, then he is not a Jew.
　　　　　　　　—Ashley Montagu, *Man's Most Dangerous Myth*

YEARS AGO I ACCOMPANIED MY BROTHER, GILLES, AND A YOUNG COU-
ple with two little boys on a hike in Point Reyes National Sea-
shore, 25 miles north of San Francisco. The mother of the two
boys, who knew that Gilles and I had escaped from Nazi France
during World War II, asked us: "Why did you escape? Was it because you were Jewish?" Gilles answered very quickly: "I am,
but my brother is not."

I was amazed at his response because a few years before he
would have simply replied: "Yes, we are Jews." Such an answer
is consistent with the idea that Jewishness is inherited. From a
racial perspective, because Gilles and I are born of the same
parents, either both or neither of us is Jewish. That concept was
pounded into our brains during our youth by racial propagan-
dists. It took years to rid myself of this false and deadly idea. On
that afternoon in California had Gilles finally realized that being
a Jew was a personal choice and not, as we were told, due to a
specific biological characteristic, like maleness of femaleness, inherited from one's parents?

My brother's answer was also astonishing for another reason.
He knew I did not consider myself a Jew. But why does he consider himself Jewish? After all, we shared the same background.
We were both reared without religion, went to the same schools,
lived under the Nazi occupation during World War II, escaped together from France, and served in the Air Force the same
amount of time. Does Gilles consider himself a Jew because of a
vague sensibility made up of various ideas, memories, and emo-

tions, together with a feeling of solidarity toward men, women, and children who were persecuted as Jews? Possibly.

Like Ashley Montagu, I define a Jew as someone who professes the Jewish religion. This implies that anyone who does not profess the Jewish religion is not a Jew. It also implies that a Jew who abandons the Jewish faith for any reason is a former Jew. Many of my friends agree with such a definition but tell me I am fighting a nonexistent battle. They say that except for the neo-Nazis of today, few would argue with me. Unfortunately, the idea that Jewishness is inherited did not die with the defeat of Germany in 1945. Today, it is anchored in the mind not only of anti-Semites, but also of other people, including Jews. Perhaps the most outstanding example is found in the book by Ellen Jaffe McClain, *Embrace the Stranger*, which reports that a Jewish woman said in a social gathering that "her brother was not [religiously] Jewish, but since both of his parents were Jewish, he was 100 percent genetically Jewish."[1]

I wonder how many genes are involved in the inheritance of Jewishness. One of my friends jokingly suggests that only one pair of genes is involved, and if Jewishness is dominant (an obvious assumption for anti-Semites), a geneticist might state that the woman and her brother are JJ. If the brother marries a non-Jewish woman, his wife is jj and his children will be Jj, that is, *half-Jews*. If one of his children marries another half-Jew, out of four children, one will be a Jew, two half-Jew, and one non-Jew. Because Jewishness is supposed to be dominant in this scheme, the genetically half-Jews will act like Jews. We should not joke, because being labeled a Jew was of deadly importance to potential Holocaust victims. Among them were a substantial number of agnostics, Christians, and members of other non-Jewish affiliations. Their "crime" was to be the child or the grandchild of someone who was or had been a Jew.

My definition of a Jew as someone who follows the Jewish faith, with the corollary that a person who does not follow the Jewish faith is not a Jew, is at variance not only with the Nazi definition, but also with the one used by many rabbis. Under traditional Jewish law a person born to a Jewish mother is a Jew. This raises the question of whether a person whose father is Jewish, but whose mother is not, is a Jew. The answer has varied with time. Recently, at least in the United States, the definition has been widened to include individuals whose father is Jewish. The idea of being a Jew because one parent is Jewish seems to me a belief in the hereditary nature of Jewishness. Is there some basis for this?

Let us consider how Orthodox rabbis view a proselyte. Proselytes are declared newborns who, through the performance of prescribed rituals, are transformed into members of the Jewish community, not only spiritually but also physically. To underscore this total transformation, the rabbis emphasize that proselytes automatically divest themselves of all their family ties and hence have no "blood" relatives whatsoever. Because of their total rebirth, the proselytes are technically considered physical descendants of the Jewish patriarchs and, in their prayers, are supposed to recite benedictions that refer to "our forefathers Abraham, Isaac, and Jacob," as do Jews who are born into a Jewish family. Therefore, for Orthodox rabbis, it seems that to be a Jew requires more than the practice of Jewish rites: one must be a descendant of Jews, at least in spirit. By insisting that a cultural trait, Jewishness, is inherited, the Jews themselves may have contributed to the idea that they belong to an exclusive family, a distinct race.

It is not astonishing to find references to the Jewish race in many books written by Jews and non-Jews toward the end of the nineteenth century when the concept of human races was at its peak. However, what is hard to understand is that the myth of the Jewish race remained alive and well in the minds of writers after World War II, especially among those who fought anti-Semitism. For example, in the introduction to a 1945 symposium against anti-Semitism, Mark Visniak wrote that ". . . antisemitism by its duration and persistence overshadows similar experiences of all other *races* [italics added]."[2] More recently, writers still seem to consider the Jews a race. For example, in 1973, Simon Wiesenthal wrote in *Sails of Hope*, "Spaniards were encouraged to feel superior to Jews, Moors, and other *races* [italics added]."[3] In Chaim Lipschitz's *Franco, Spain, the Jews, and the Holocaust*, written in 1984, one finds this sentence: "The Sephardim were spared economic ruin which faced many others of their *race*" [italics added].[4] Paul Johnson uses the word "race" in *A History of the Jews*.[5] John Lynch writes in a chapter entitled "Spain after the Expulsion," that Alejandro Maria Aguado, banker to the court of Ferdinand VII and the financier Juan Alvarez Mendizabal were *"Jewish by race, catholic in religion* [italics added], throwbacks to the *conversos* of Philip IV."[6] Alex Bein uses "race" more than once in *The Jewish Question*,[7] and believes that Jews can be recognized by external characteristics.[8] Throughout *Bound Upon a Wheel of Fire*, Jon Dipell weds the word "race" to Jews.[9] In *Jews in China*, Sidney Shapiro constantly used the word 'race' in relation to Jews.[10] Michel Abitol in *The Jews of North Africa during the Second World War* put quotations around the word *race* in relation to the Jews, but does not explain why.[11] The last chapter of Jon Gager's book, *The Origins of Antisemitism*, is entitled, "What is the Heart of Paul's argument with the Jews, his kinsmen by race?"[12] What does Gager mean by "race"?

Many Jewish and non-Jewish writers find it difficult to accept the idea that Judaism is simply a religion and Jews who abandon the Jewish faith, whether they adopt another religion or not at all, are no longer Jews. For example, one finds in *Antisemitism in the Contemporary World*, edited by Michael Curtis, the following: "French Jews were most non-observant."[13] If they are not observant, then they are not Jews. In *De l'antijudaisme à l'antisémitisme contemporain*, Paul Colongue wrote:

> The first German national assembly will include several Jews, but will elect as its first president, Eduard Simson, a Jew (converted to Protestantism), who in 1871, would become the president of the First Reichstag.[14]

Because Simson was converted to Protestantism, he was no longer a Jew. Other writers make similar statements. In *Antisemitism*, Leon Poliakov uses the term "non-practicing Jews."[15] If they are not practicing Jews, they are not Jews. In his book, *The Conquerors*, Michael Beschloss makes the same mistake. He wrote: "Bernard Baruch, the Wall Street tycoon, self-styled advisor to Presidents, and a non-practicing Jew."[16]

David Gerber writes in *Antisemitism in American History*, "Whether Jews are rich or poor, radical or conservatives, powerful or impotent, religious or secular"[17] What does he mean by secular? If he means non-religious, then these people are not Jews. In an outstanding scholarly book *Antisemitism in America*, Leonard Dimmerstein described Theobald of Canterbury as a Jew who converted to Christianity.[18] Dimmerstein should have written "a former Jew", as did Todd Endelmam in *Radical Assimilation in English Jewish History*[19] or Nora Levin in *The Jews in the Soviet Union since 1917*.[20] Levin was not consistent, however; she also wrote, page 25: "The Jews whom Lenin knew best, Gregori Zinovie, Leon Trostky, Yuli Narov, and Leon Keamenev, were wholly russified and represented prototypes of the Jews to be." If "wholly russified" means they had abandoned any religious faith, then they were no longer Jews.

Journalists also find it difficult to accept the idea that Judaism is a religion, not a race. In a recent issue of the *New York Times Magazine* I found the following, "Mr. Spiegel also said he would try to continue the unfinished work of reconciling *Germans and Jews* [italics added]."[21] Does the person who said this imply that Jews in Germany are not German? At issue is the task of reconciling Jews and non-Jews.

The Vatican also has difficulty in accepting the idea that Jewishness is a religion and the corollary that Jews who become Catholics are no longer Jews. In recent statements it labels as "Jews" those men and women who converted to Catholicism during the Nazi period. It has been suggested that such statements may be inspired largely by a desire to clean up the image of the Roman Catholic hierarchy tarnished during World War II.[22] To call these new converts Jews reflects a definition of the Jews that may be used by others for racist purposes. The Vatican should refer to them as converted Jews.

The idea that Jews remain Jews, even if they abandon the Jewish faith, is also found among demographers who study Jewish populations. For example, the National Jewish Population Survey (NJPS) states that there are about 5.5 million Jews in the United States.[23] The survey counts 1,310,000 people who were born into Jewish families, but who either claim no religion or adhere to another religion. Also counted in the survey are 185,000 converts. Both sets of Jews cannot be included. If religion is the criterion, Jews who have abandoned the Jewish faith must be excluded. If ancestry is the criterion, the converts with no Jewish ancestry cannot be counted.

The idea that Jews and non-Jews are biologically different persists. Consider the work of two contemporary historians, Gerald Sorin and Paula Hyman. Sorin writes:

> Indeed, if German Jews set the stage for the new immigrants, Eastern Europeans supplied the *biological* and cultural reinforcement needed to save American Jewry.[24] [italics added]

What does Sorin imply by biological reinforcement? Does he believe that Eastern Jews are biologically different from American Jews?

Hyman, discussing the problems of integration, equates intermarriage (between Jews and non-Jews) to a biological merger:

> However, French Jews were not fully integrated into French society and sought neither the disappearance of their own institution, nor their *biological merger* with the French population.[25] [italics added]

She should have written "nor intermarriage with the rest of the French population."

The title of a more recent book, *Black, Jewish, and Interracial,* written by Kayta Gibel Azoulay, implies that Jews form a race because marriage between Jews and Blacks is explored as interracial.[26]

Before I attempt to destroy the myth of the Jewish race from both a biological and historical point of view, I want to explore in some details the origins of that myth.

The Myth
of the Jewish Race

I
The History of the Concept
of the Jewish Race

Introduction to Part I

For at least two thousand years of recorded history social ac-
tions have been implemented based on the beliefs that certain people had something inherent in them, something in
their blood, that made them less human and consequently de-
serving of persecution or even death.

—Richard Lerner

THE BELIEF TO WHICH RICHARD LERNER ALLUDED IS RACISM. AMONG
its victims are the Jews, who endured centuries of persecution.
They have been falsely accused of playing a major part in killing
Jesus Christ; of polluting the wafer of the Eucharist,[1] of poison-
ing wells and fountains in order to kill as many Christians as possible; of conspiring to overthrow governments and undermine
societies; and founding two opposing economic systems, capital-
ism and communism.

An unreasonable hostility toward the Jews is generally known
as anti-Semitism,[2] although *Semitic* originally referred to certain
languages and peoples of the Eastern Mediterranean that included not only Jews but also Palestinians, Assyrians, Babylonians, and Phoenicians. Some writers make a distinction
between the terms "anti-Judaism" and "anti-Semitism".[3] The
former is hatred of the Jews based on religious grounds; the latter, on the idea that Jews are an inferior and unworthy "race."
According to these writers, when the Catholic Church lost some
of its power and the middle classes emerged in the eighteenth
century, anti-Judaism was transformed into anti-Semitism. I believe the distinction between these terms is correct, but I am
convinced that anti-Semitism appeared in Spain as early as the
seventh century.[4]

Although many Spanish Jews converted to Christianity, they
continued to be persecuted because the Spanish did not believe
they could ever be true Christians, that is, *Judaism was in their*

25

blood. This is ironic because the first Christians were Jews, and the Catholic Church was founded by a Jew.

The belief that Jews were a distinct race was unknown in antiquity,[5] but was well established by the Middle Ages. Jews were considered biologically distinct as early as the thirteenth century. They were said to have specific physical characteristics, such as hooked noses, twitching eyelids, clenched teeth, protruding ears, square fingernails, flat feet, and round knees. Because all Jews were assumed to have these characteristics, the inference was that they were a distinct race. Anti-Semitism did not disappear even during the Enlightenment, with its principles of rationalism, humanism, and universalism.

Race science burgeoned during the late nineteenth century and early twentieth century and gave support to the idea that Jews belonged to a distinct and inferior race. Race science is the study of human differences based on "demonstrable" anthropological, biological, and statistical proofs.[6] This pseudo-science was developed and applied by anthropologists in large part to justify European imperialism.

Although the violent nature of anti-Semitism has a very long history, Hitler carried persecution to its extreme with the "Final Solution." The Nazi Holocaust and its horrors were an attempt to eliminate the whole "Jewish race." There is a vast literature and documentation on this subject, but little has been written to dispel the myth of a Jewish race. Contrary to common belief, Jews cannot be physically identified as Jews. For this reason, in the Middle Ages, they were required to wear identifying marks such as the *rouelle* (a circular insignia) in the Latin countries or conical hats in Germany. Later attempts to identify Jews also failed. During the Nazi period, experts who supposedly could recognize Jews within the population according to scientific clues, roamed the streets and public places in search of them. Because positive identification was impossible, many whose looks did not conform the preconceived Nazi idea of Jewish appearance escaped the hunt,[7] whereas others, mostly children, who were not Jewish were arrested and eliminated because they "looked Jewish."[8]

The difficulty that the Nazis encountered is similar to that of biologists and anthropologists who try to classify mankind into racial groups. Decades of effort have failed. The idea that there

are no distinct human races has gained acceptance with anthropologists only in the last twenty years, and the public at large is
not aware of this recent scientific conclusion. The terms "race"
and "racial" still appear in newspapers, magazines, and political
speeches as well as in legal rulings. Race is still used in crime
and health statistics, as a factor in sentencing criminals, and on
college and university admission forms.[9]

Such views may not be surprising in the general public, but it
is astonishing to find them in the writing of modern scholars who
study anti-Semitism.[10] The continuous use of such terms indicates that many people, Jews and non-Jews alike, still believe,
consciously or unconsciously, that Jews constitute a distinct
race.

1

The Jewish Race: From Antiquity to the Middle Ages

I. The Ancient World

> Neither racial anti-Semitism, invention of modern pedants, nor the economic anti-Semitism, product of legislation in the Middle Ages and of modern judgment of financial monopoly, nor religious intolerance played an appreciable role in the time of the Greco-Roman Empire.
>
> —Theodore Reinach
> *Textes d'auteurs Grecs et Romains relatif au Judaism* (1894)
> [Translation by the author]

THERE IS A CONSENSUS AMONG HISTORIANS THAT ANTI-SEMITISM, AS we know it today, did not exist in the ancient world.[1] The notion of "race" was unknown to the ancients,[2] and although the word appears in French, German, and English translations of their works, they used the term "nation" or "people." The translators may have been influenced by the prevailing racism of their own time.[3] In 1967 Sherwin White published a series of papers he delivered in Cambridge, *Racial Prejudice in Imperial Rome*. This title is confusing because, as White himself suggests,[4] the examples of prejudice that he gives concern not the "race" but the nation and especially the culture of other peoples.

Racial distinctions were not used in ancient times, at least not to point out special physical characteristics of people. Greek and Roman writers did not use physical attributes to ridicule Jews and they did not ascribe to the notion of a Jewish race in a biological sense. A Jew was a person who practiced Judaism. There was no finality in being a Jew. The proselyte was a Jew; the apos-

tate was no longer a Jew.[5] The distinction between Jews and
non-Jews was political, social, religious, or national but never racial. That Jews could be biologically different did not enter the
mind of the ancients who saw around them many people who had
converted to Judaism and many Jews who had abandoned their
faith and married non-Jews.

In the ancient world hatred of Jews was more a literary than a
popular phenomenon.[6] The inferiority of people based on racial
grounds is absent in the writings of Tacitus and Cicero. Although
both authors make many derogatory statements about the Jews,
nevertheless, they do not remark on outward traits to ridicule
them as a race or characterize them as inferior people who cannot be "romanized." There was hostility against Jews,[7] in part
because of their belief in one God, in contrast to the polytheism
prevalent in antiquity, and in part because they considered themselves to be the Chosen People, which implied superiority to others. This attitude is still present among some Jews, and I know
two highly educated Jewish men who believe that Jews are intellectually superior to non-Jews.

The Greeks and Romans reproached the Jews for living apart,
for not sharing their food, for not participating in games or military duties, and for not honoring the same laws.[8] Many peoples
were conquered by the Romans, and exiled from their homeland
and gradually assimilated with their neighbors, but most Jews
did not. They kept their customs and religion as free as possible
of foreign influence. The more the Jews kept themselves apart,
the greater was the hostility toward them. The first seeds of hatred were sown among the peoples with whom the Jews lived.[9]

The ancients may have resented the Jews, but they believed
that the Jews could change their habits and customs and in
doing so lose their separate identity. This is an important point,
because anti-Semites today believe firmly that Jews cannot assimilate—once a Jew, always a Jew. This belief is also held by
some orthodox Jews.

In brief, the Greco-Roman Empire included people of highly diverse customs and beliefs and discrimination as we know it did
not exist. In this pluralistic world, Jews had the same professions
as the people among whom they lived. They were farmers, arti-
sans, and craftsmen who earned their living by the sweat of their
brow.[10] They were not necessarily merchants or physicians, as

they would become later. In other words, Jews did not differ from their neighbors except in their religion and traditional customs.

Once Christianity was recognized as the official religion, pluralism disappeared, and life for the Jews became very difficult.[11] Among other restrictions, they were forbidden to own land and slaves. Forced to live in the cities, they turned to commerce. Rabbinical jurisdiction or the right of Jews to administer justice among themselves was abolished or greatly reduced. Proselytism became punishable by death. Jews were excluded from military careers and from holding high offices.[12] This kind of discrimination eventually spread throughout Europe.

II. The Middle Ages

In the Ancient world antisemitism was more a literary than a popular form, whereas in the Middle Ages the masses of the people were imbued with hatred of the Jews in proportion as the Church through rites and education inspired them with her view of the Jews as a race accursed of God.

—Hugo Valentin
Antisemitism

Many historians distinguish between Catholic anti-Judaism and racial anti-Semitism in the nineteenth and twentieth centuries,[13] but others maintain that the demarcation disappeared far earlier. According to James Caroll and Julio Caro Baroja[14] anti-Semitism had its roots in Spain when the Inquisition targeted Jewish converts to Christianity strictly on the basis of "their impure blood."[15] Benzion Netanyahu believes that racial antisemitism originated in Spain in the seventh century.[16]

Today, it is difficult to accept the idea that Jews are biologically different from Christians. During the Middle Ages, however, the Christian masses were largely illiterate, steeped in superstition, and thus easily misled. Many stories of the time portrayed the Jews as evil. For hundreds of years, Christians falsely accused them of many crimes. It was said that Jewish doctors were magicians who tore the heart out of Christian children to use in healing Jewish patients. Jews not only were blamed for the death of Jesus, but also were the victims of heinous and malevolent slanders. For example, it was said that every year at Passover, they slew a Christian for their feast, used sorcery, adored donkeys, poisoned wells, tortured Christian children, and even sacrificed their own sons and daughters to Satan.[17]

Jews as the agents of the Devil were often the subject of sermons by local and itinerant priests. Some of these remain in the Christian catechism today. The better known are by St. John Chrysostom, one of the most virulent Jew-haters of the fourth century. Other preachers whose words against the Jews are immortalized in sacred Christian books are Gregory of Nyssa (306–31) and St. Augustine of Hippo (354–430). In the ninth century, Agobard, Archbishop of Lyon, the second largest city in France, wrote pamphlets that refer to Jews as sons of Satan. He accused them of raping Christian women, and kidnaping Christian children to sell them to Muslims as slaves. Hundreds of copies of these pamphlets were made in the monasteries and used as sermons to illiterate congregations for many generations after Agobard's death.[18]

During the tenth and eleventh centuries the word "Devil" was so closely associated with the word "Jew" as to be almost synonymous. Judaism was regarded not as another religion, but as an antireligion, that is, in opposition to Christianity. To kill a Jew was to destroy the Devil. Stories were told, sermons preached, songs sung, and pictures painted about the Devil-Jew.

Until the thirteenth century, Jews were depicted as normal human beings, but beginning in 1215, portraits changed. In large paintings of New Testament figures, the Apostles, church fathers, and saints were portrayed as clean-cut, graceful, innocent individuals, with noble features and shining countenance. In contrast, the model for the anti-Christ was the Jew, who was pictured as grotesque, with an exaggerated hooked nose, frequently with horns protuding from his head, and sometimes with a tail and a beard resembling those of a goat.

Jews were portrayed as less than human in tapestries, in drawings, and other forms of art. They were made nonhuman because that is how many Christians imagined them. One of the most outlandish fables was the notion that Jewish men menstruated and therefore required Christian blood to replenish themselves.[19] Although Christianity postdated Judaism, the fable did not explain where the Jews got the blood they needed before there were any Christians.

Another source of discrimination may have begun in 1215 when the fourth Lateran Council required Jews to wear distinctive insignia on their clothing. The difference in dress contributed to the belief that Jews were physically different from non-Jews. According to Leon Poliakov:

> this stigma became the accepted attribute of the unconverted Jew. In the fourteenth century, artists and illuminators rarely represented them otherwise, even when portraying Biblical Jews, patriarchs of the old testament. By a remarkable osmosis, these views took root even among the Jews themselves, certain of whose manuscripts of the fourteenth and fifteen centuries represent Abraham, Jacob, and Moses in the same costume. This visible sign which henceforth indicates the circumcised, impresses on men's mind the notion that the Jews was a man of another physical aspect, radically different from other men.[20]

Slowly, but surely, the original idea that Jews differed from Christians only in their religious beliefs gave way to the notion that they were biologically different, that they were another type of human beings, and belonged to another race. This transformation can be summarized as follows. First, the Jews were seen as the agents of the Devil. Then, they were assumed to be sons of the Devil with some diabolical attributes. Once they were dehumanized, they had to be biologically different, and they could not be saved by conversion or assimilation, because their wickedness was passed from one generation to the next through their blood. Spanish racial anti-Semitism had its origin in this new concept of inherited wrong, the subject of the next chapter.

2

Spain and the Concept of the Jewish Race

It was in Castille, where the Conversos' rapid rise to power on municipal councils coincided with the intensification of the struggle between the disenfranchised popular classes and the municipal oligarchy, that a virulent form of anti-Semitism emerged.

—Stephen Haliczer
Inquisition and Society in the Kingdom of Valencia, 1471–1834

THE MOST SUCCESSFUL RACIST GOVERNMENTAL PROGRAM BEFORE the Nazi period was the one carried out by the Spanish Inquisition. The target was the Jews who had converted to Christianity and their descendants. Many were burned at the stake, very often on the trumped-up charge that they were still practicing the Jewish faith. These converts and their descendants are customarily called Conversos, New Christians, or Marranos.[1]

According to Benzion Netanyahu a deep rift between Ibero-Romans and the Jewish community already existed in the fifth century.[2] It gradually broadened into the proportions of a gulf, as the Jewish population increased in Spanish society, which regarded Jews as foreigners. The Third Toledo Council enacted laws in 589 to limit the activity of the Jews.[3] Jewish men were prohibited from buying Christian slaves and marrying Christian women. Children born to Jewish–Christian parents had to be baptized as Christians. A few years later, forced conversions of all age groups became the rule.

In 633 the Fourth Toledo Council ruled that Jews who married Christians must convert. "Jews and those who are of the Jews" were debarred from public office. This discrimination was not only religious but also racial because it was aimed at descendants of Jews who had become Christians. The law was based on the assumption that they could not be trusted because of their Jewish ancestry. The evil of Jewishness was in their " blood." I do not know if this was the first case of official racial discrimination in the world, but there is little doubt that racial discrimination in Spain against the Conversos had its roots in the seventh century.[4]

In 711 a large part of Spain was conquered by the Arabs, and the Spanish Jews (and Conversos) entered a period of grace, known as the *Convivencia*. As long as Spain was under Islam, Jews enjoyed a relative tolerance. This period was interrupted in 1148, when Spain was invaded by the Almoravides, a fanatic and intolerant North African Muslim sect. Many Jews took refuge in the Christian lands of Castile, Aragon, Languedoc, and Provence. The Convivencia broke down completely during the thirteenth century, when the Christians began the conquest of Muslim Spain in earnest.[5] With the Reconquest, both Jews and Muslims came under pressure to convert to Catholicism, but the Jews suffered far more than the Muslims from intolerance and persecution. In 1391 a tide of hatred culminated in a widespread and horrifying massacre of Jews. Popular assaults were carried out against a large number of Jewish communities, many of which did not survive.

To escape persecution many Jews converted to Christianity, but the popular antipathy toward the Jews was soon transferred to the Conversos, who as New Christians were eligible for government positions. Many of them became tax collectors, an office that was widely hated particularly by the lower ranks of Spanish society. The hatred heightened during the fourteenth century when Spain was struck by a series of economic and other catastrophes, including the Black Death. The nobility also scorned and detested the New Christians, partly for the same reasons and because of jealousy: conversos could be judges, bishops, and other ranking officers and even could marry daughters of the aristocracy.

The Spanish people, whose feelings became more and more inflamed, saw in the conversos only hypocritical Jews who had lost none of their "evil attributes." Demands increased that the conversos be separated from other believers, but Catholic doctrine prevented any such distinction. A conversion, even forced, was deemed irrevocable and baptism was indelible. Hence, discrimination had to be based on the same grounds used a few centuries before: Jewish ancestry, not professed religious belief, was the key to decreasing the power of the conversos. Although thousands of them had only the dimmest memories of ancestral religion by this time, in the eyes of "Old Christians," they bore the stigma of their origins. They were "Jews," and should be treated as such, with appropriately diminished rights.

A movement arose to create an organization that would eliminate anyone who deviated from the true faith. In 1478, King Ferdinand of Aragon and Queen Isabel of Castile, under political pressure, petitioned the pope to establish inquisitional tribunals, and the request was granted in 1481.Three main reasons were given for the foundation of the Inquisition: the political decision to achieve religious conformity in Spain, the striking failure of enforced conversion of the Jewish and Moorish populations, and a profound fear that insincere converts would contaminate the Christian faith. To prevent such contamination, the Inquisition was charged to weed out of society all conversos suspected of secretly practicing Jewish rites.[6] This would be achieved by investigating not only personal behavior, but also genealogies for the taint of Jewishness.

Most probably the real purpose of the Inquisition was to remove the conversos from their influential positions and to legalize confiscation of their possessions which were scrupulously inventoried, but never returned.[7] The confiscation helped fill empty royal coffers often depleted by Ferdinand's costly wars. The heretics targeted by the Inquisition were the richest men and women in the city, and King Ferdinand and Queen Isabel divided the appropriated wealth into three parts. The first part went to pay the costs of the Inquisition itself; the second part to the royal coffers for the wars against the Moors in Granada; the third part to religious works, such as building new churches and monasteries.[8]

The conversos became the object of a nationwide hunt. No matter how carefully they tried to conform to the behavior expected of "true" Catholics, they were members of the despised "Jewish race," which had to be checked or exterminated. Although a large number escaped persecution and are the ancestors of many men and women living today in Spain, quite a few were tortured and burned at the stake or were forced to emigrate. The Jews were expelled from Spain in 1492 and the Muslims forced out between 1609 and 1614; however conversos and Moriscos (converted Muslims) remained victims of the Inquisition until the beginning of the nineteenth century. It is ironic that the conversos were victimized to a far greater extent than the Jews, because they or their ancestors had become Christians in order to escape the exclusions and persecution to which Jews were subjected. My interpretation is that the Jews were victims of anti-Judaism, and they were persecuted for what they believed, which is religious persecution, whereas the conversos were persecuted not for what they believed, but for being descendants of Jews—which is racial persecution.

It appears that in Spain the word *race* took on its modern meaning: a group of people biologically distinct from all others. The word is of Hebrew or Arabic origin and originally denoted descendants of a single sire, especially when referring to animals. It later was applied to human beings, as in the phrase "the race of Abraham."[9] Jewish and non-Jewish writers used the term *razza* for Jews as well as for conversos and Moriscos, to distinguish them from members of the older Christian community.

For example, Antonio de Montoro wrote to Juan Poeta:

We belong to the same race; you and I are Jews. The offenses done to you are mine; the shame I suffer is yours.[10]

The chronicler Ibn Verga wrote in 1391: It is not even certain that a thousandth of the race of the Jews still survive.[11] The word *race* also appears in the text of an accusation against six Jews and five conversos that they tried to ruin Christendom through black magic.[12] There is also reference to the Jewish race in a note to Charles V: "We inform the King and the Queen that within their kingdom there are many Christians of the Jewish race who practice the Jewish faith in secret.[13]

The Spanish use of *race* when referring to Jews and Moors gave broader implications to what were essentially religious differences. To equate societal groups with breeding lines of animals, even symbolically, suggests not only that religious differences are biologically transmitted from one generation to the next but also that race is instrumental in the formation of our qualities and mental constitution. The conversos, who were offspring of Jews, were assumed to retain the "racial" mental make-up of their ancestors and therefore should be treated as Jews.

It is ironic that both Isabel and Ferdinand, responsible for the establishment of the Inquisition, had Jewish ancestry, he from his mother's side, she from her father's side.[14] Whatever they thought about their " tainted blood," we will never know. Why did they support a program that made them possible targets? Did they feel, like the Grand Inquisitor and converso Tomas de Torquemada,[15] that they had to attack in order to demonstrate their Christian orthodoxy? Did they have the Machiavelian idea of using the Inquisition against the middle and upper classes who had intermarried with conversos over the last ten decades in order to centralize their royal authority?[16] Whatever the reason, the result was clearly a preview of the Holocaust.

In Spain, as in Germany centuries later, Jewishness was considered an inheritable biological characteristic. One drop of "Jewish blood" was enough to make someone inferior, a person who could not be trusted, who could be discriminated against, persecuted, and even put to death. In both countries, centuries apart, it was believed that Jews possessed a defect which was passed from one generation to another, either through human blood or human milk. In 1681 the Grand Inquisitor, Vallardes, could not find a blemish in the ancestry of an heretic he was examining. Vallardes established that the man's wet nurse had Jewish ancestors and therefore had corrupted him as a child through her milk.[17] This recalls a memorandum in the archives of the Ministry of Justice of the Third Reich:

> After the birth of a child, a *pure blooded* Jewess sold her mother milk to a pediatrician, hiding the fact that she was Jewish. Babies of *German blood* were nourished on this milk in a maternity hospital. The accused woman will be tried for fraud. The purchasers of the milk have been wronged, for the milk of a Jewish woman cannot be considered nourishment for German children.[18] (Emphasis added)

Both the Grand Inquisitor and the official in the German Ministry of Justice believed that Jewish contamination could be transmissible from wet nurse to child. Jewishness to them was as infectious as the AIDS virus is today.

This astonishing example illustrates how the rationale for hating Jews shifted from religion to race. Alonso de Espina, a Franciscan priest who helped to convince the authorities to establish the Inquisition, argued: "Jews and Conversos are one and the same people—a race. If Jews were a race, there could not be such a thing as a Jew who becomes a Christian."[19] In his mind, baptism could convert an individual from one religious faith to another, but could not make a converso a true Spaniard. Centuries later a similar idea was prevalent in Nazi Germany: Jews converted to Christianity could never become "true" Germans.

The idea of de Espina became part of the justification for the Inquisition. A distinction was drawn between Old and New Christians. The latter were the descendants—even half a dozen generations or more—of those who had accepted baptism, but were to be treated as a race apart. For example, children were designated by the Inquisition as being "half" or "one-quarter" New Christian. Occasionally still more gradations were recorded.[20] A similar classification was used under the Nazis, based on Aryan race rather than on religion. Both classifications are nonsensical from a biological point of view since Christianity is not a biological trait and the Aryan race is a myth.

The idea that Jewishness is biologically inheritable was pounded into Spanish people during the Middle Ages just as it would be among the Germans and to a lesser degree the French centuries later. It should be noted, however, that Spanish racism was even more extreme than the Nazi brand. In Spain a person with a single Jewish ancestor, however remote, was discriminated against; in Hitler's Germany a person with only one Jewish grandparent was spared. Racist propaganda vilifying the Jews and their descendants was used effectively for political purposes in both countries. Henry II used such vilification to dethrone his half-brother, Peter I of Castile.[21] Five hundred years later Adolph Stocker used it to gain a seat in the Prussian Chamber of deputies.[22]

Other parallels can be drawn between Christian Spain and Nazi Germany. The first anti-Jewish legislation passed by the Nazis prevented Jews from holding certain public positions. They could not be judges, educators, members of city councils, and so on. In Spain as early as the seventh century, conversos could not hold public offices. In order to keep the Old and New

Christians apart, laws to maintain purity of (Christian) blood, known as *Limpezia de Sangre*, were instituted. "Pure blood" was a requirement in Spain and Portugal for holding political and ecclesiatical office, to be a judge, or an educator. Many people sought certificates of "purity" as proofs that they did not have Jewish or Moorish ancestors, and these certificates were a major source of revenue for the Church.[23] In similar fashion, many Jews escaped death during World War II by forging family papers.

Furthermore, the savagery with which the Spanish Inquisition attacked the New Christians and the Nazis attacked the Jews was similar. Both branded their victims as outcasts, confiscated their possessions, incarcerated them, killed them, robbed their descendants of their rightful inheritance, or subjected them to a reign of terror which turned their lives into something worse than death. One difference was that in Spain the conversos were systematically tortured to produce confessions of guilt. In Nazi Europe there was no such need, since simply being a Jew was sufficient.[24]

In conclusion, Spanish conversos were victims of a racism similar to that which dominated Europe in the first half of the twentieth century. Although baptized as Catholics, they were still considered Jews. The criterion of Jewishness no longer hinged on religion, but on ancestry. Hatred of Jews had shifted from religious to racial bigotry.[25]

3
Science and the Concept of the Jewish Race

THE RENAISSANCE WAS A VERY IMPORTANT STEP IN THE CULTURAL evolution of humanity. It was more than a revival of art, literature, and science under the classical models of Greco-Roman civilization. It was a time when traditions were shaken by the interest in new things, often simply because they were new. In an era of reason one would expect less emphasis on the idea of human races, but on the contrary, scholars assumed that there were multiple types (races) of humans and attempted to classify them. Despite their best efforts, they were unsuccessful. They should have abandoned their preconceived motions, but they did not. By ignoring the lack of evidence they became bad scientists. One example of bad science has to do with Jews.

I. THE ENLIGHTENMENT

The World's great men have not commonly been great scholars, nor its great scholars great men.
—Oliver Wendell Holmes

The discovery of populations different from themselves led Europeans to doubt whether all mankind descended of only one couple. Once the fundamental biblical assumption about Adam and Eve was questioned, scholars began to debate other aspects of the received wisdom. For the first time since the Greeks, they attacked preconceived notions and prohibitions based upon doctrine and dogma and labored to free the intellect from the myths and fanaticism that have enslaved it for centuries. This was the beginning of the Age of Enlightenment.

With regard to preconceived notions about the Jews, however, the results were less than enlightened. The principles of the Enlightenment were rationalism, humanism, and universalism. According to all these principles, a Jew should have been regarded like anyone else. Rationalism declared that reason was the highest authority and did not permit an individual's status to be based on religious tenets. Humanism demanded respect for the human element in every person. Universalism prescribed that the rights of all men be determined by uniform criteria.

A few writers of the Enlightenment condemned the ever constant persecution of the Jews. Among them were Pierre Bayle,[1] Charles Montesquieu,[2] Jean Jacques Rousseau,[3] and the Humboldt brothers, Wilhelm and Alexander, who perceived humanity as a whole without distinction of religion and color.[4] These authors were of sufficient stature to influence the French revolutionaries in 1790 and 1791 to emancipate the Jews, not as a community but as individuals. There was no sympathy among the French revolutionaries for Judaism, which they viewed along with Catholicism as barbarous superstition. According to Robert Wistrich:

> For them, the Old Testament was no less obnoxious than the Gospel, the Synagogue no less offensive to reason than the Church, and rabbis as much imposters as priests. Indeed these rationalists, who were sworn enemies of the Church were often disposed to see the source of its intolerance, fanaticism, and superstition in the Hebrew bible and the teachings of Judaism.[5]

These attacks on Judaism inflamed hostilities. Hatred of Jews, instead of disappearing with the Enlightenment, was simply given a new "rational" basis no less pernicious than the irrational ones it replaced. To their traditional crimes was now added their "fossilized" religion, which was an obstacle to human progress.

Among the French philosophers Voltaire was the most virulent anti-Semite. Although known for fighting intolerance and bigotry, he wrote the following about Jews:

> We find in them only an ignorant and barbarous people, who have long united the most sordid avarice with the most detestable superstition and the most invincible hatred for every people by whom they are tolerated and enriched.[6]

The same idea was expressed by Paul Henry Thiry d'Holbach in *Système de La Nature:*

> Dare, therefore, O Europe, to shake off at last the unbearable yoke of the prejudices which afflict thee! Leave these superstitions, as debased as they are senseless to stupid Hebrews, to fanatic imbeciles, to craven and degraded Asians. They are not made for the inhabitants of thy climes . . . close thy eyes forever to such vain chimera, which for many centuries have served only to delay progress toward true science and to divert thee from the paths of happiness.[7]

Jews were to be denied any share in the rights inherent in the principles of rationalism, humanism, and universalism. To many, the ideals of the Enlightenment did not apply to the Jews.[8]

A view prevalent at the time was polygenesis, the belief that mankind has separate origins and that human "races" were created separately. An early advocate was John Atkins, an Englishman, who was persuaded that the "Black and White Races had sprung from different colored First Parents.[9] Polygenesis was opposed to religious orthodoxy and for that reason it attracted philosophers like Voltaire, who elevated it to the status of scientific theory. The belief in polygenesis was not universal, but most everyone thought that there were varieties or races of human beings who differed not only physically, but also mentally. These assumptions were accepted by later "scientists," who attempted to classify mankind. "Race science" was thus born from the Enlightenment prejudices, and the Jews were to be one of its primary victims.

II. THE JEWS: VICTIMS OF BAD SCIENCE

Part 1

> The notion that Jews are a separate distinct race took hold in the century after the French Revolution, as biology and anthropology moved to provide the basis of a distinction which French law no longer permitted.
>
> —Michael Marrus
> *The Politics of Assimilation*

Anti-Semitism existed in Europe well before the eighteenth century, it took firm hold after the French Revolution. Before

1789, the French Jewish community was a nation within a nation with its own laws. The Revolution granted Jews citizenship, but they had to give up claims to national, communal, and judicial separateness.[10] Their enemies could no longer argue that they were foreigners and could not easily invoke the claim that they were hostile to Christians, because now France had become a secular nation. The Catholic Church had lost a great deal of power, sharing blame with the monarchy and the nobility for the terrible conditions under which most of the French had lived. Later, during the Napoleonic wars, Jews in other Western European nations also were granted citizenship.

In this new political climate, another basis had to be found on which to attack the Jews and allies merged among scientists interested in human classification. In 1735, Carl Linné, the father of taxonomy, divided human beings into four groups:

Europeanus or white: light, lively, inventive, ruled by rites;
Americanus or red: tenacious, contented, free, ruled by customs;
Asiaticus or yellow: stern, haughty, stingy, ruled by opinion;
Africanus or black: cunning, slow, negligent, ruled by caprice

Linné arbitrarily linked behavioral and moral characteristics to an observable physical trait, skin color. Furthermore, he assumed that these characteristics were exclusive to each group and shared by all its members. He assigned the most desirable aspects to "whites," and the least desirable to Negroes. In so doing, he introduced elements of racism into science, which many still do not question.[11]

The study of human diversity based on the idea of human races is known as race science. The basic assumptions are (1) each human race possesses a specific set of unique physical characteristics; (2) the unique physical characteristics are linked to unique behavioral characteristics; and (3) human races are by nature unequal and can be ranked in order of intellectual, moral, and cultural superiority.

Race scientists spent many years taking physical measurements in an effort to classify peoples into distinct races. They failed because the original assumptions had no basis in fact. They were bad scientists because they did not ask the proper question: Are there physical characteristics which unequivocally divide humans into distinct races? Instead they sought to prove the assumption that there are human races. They attempted to document the specific qualities of each "racial" group as held by popular belief. They paid close attention to hair color and eye color; the shape of the head, chin, and nose; and other assumed indicators of race identity. In the process they invented a variety of techniques to measure even minuscule differences in features, none of which proved to be useful.

Race scientists have been rightly accused of making inferences from inadequate samples of individuals and even consciously or unconsciously altering their data.[12] They also spread pseudo-facts, such as interracial sterility (the offspring of a "black" and "white" couple cannot reproduce) and interspecific reproduction (apes and humans can have viable offspring.[13]

Attempts to fit the Jews into the race classification scheme demonstrate how bad this science was. If Jews were biologically different from non-Jews, race scientists should have been able to find characteristics possessed only by each group, but, they were unable to do so. They should have concluded, as good scientists would, that Jews did not belong to a separate race. Instead, they kept looking in vain for new ways to differentiate them.

At first, Jews were classified as "white." Soon, however, the white race was divided into two main branches: the Aryan and the Semitic. Jews were non-Aryan.[14] The problem with this classification is that it is rooted not in biology but in linguistics.[15] During the first half of the nineteenth century European scholars exploring the origin of languages divided them into two main groups. One has its roots in Sanskrit and was called Aryan.[16] The other sprang from ancient Hebrew and was designated as Semitic (from Shem, the second son of Noah).[17]

The jump from a linguistic to a racial classification was based on the flawed assumption that the people who speak a particular language belong to the same "racially" pure stock, and the language of a person determines his or her race. As Julian Huxley protested at the beginning of the twentieth century,[18] community of language does not prove unity of descent (Huxley may have had in mind the U.S. population). As a matter of fact, within the supposed Aryan race one finds the whole range of human characteristics assumed by race scientists to separate races: skull size, height, skin color, and so on.[19] The same can be said about the supposed Semitic race. Yet, despite their physical diversity, Jews were regarded by race scientists (mostly those in Germany) as racially pure, easily identifiable and readily distinguishable from their non-Jewish neighbors.

The alleged racial purity of Jews was based on bad science. Selective observation seemed to have been the rule. For example, the English anthropologist John Beddoe affirmed in 1861 (without statistical data) that Jews have prominent eyes, well-marked eyebrows, a receding chin, and full lips.[20] He never mentioned that many Jews do not have these characteristics and that many non-Jews do.[21]

Race scientists had two explanations for the racial purity of the Jews. Both are untrue. Jews look alike because they breed only among themselves, and their physical appearance is not affected by changes in the environment.[22] The assumption that Jews do not interbreed with non-Jews is historically untrue, as will be shown in later chapters. As for changes in climate, the appearance of all humans is unaffected. Let us explore this further.

It is well known today that when people migrate to a new location with a markedly different climate, a situation that fits the populating of Eurasia from Africa, skin color is changed by natural selection from dark to light, dark being adaptive in Africa, and light being adaptive in northern climes (see chapter 5). I say *by natural selection* because for years it was believed that skin color changes were due to a now-discarded theory of inheritance. For example, when addressing the First General Racial Congress, Felix Von Luschan said:

> We know that color of hair and skin is only the effect of the environment, and that we are fair only because our ancestors lived for thousand of years in sunless and foggy countries. Fairness is nothing else but lack of pigment, and our ancestors lost part of their pigment because they did not *need* it.[23] [emphasis added]

This argument is interesting because it is based on the Lamarckian theory of inheritance of acquired characteristics, which had been disproved by the end of the nineteenth century but obviously not yet discarded in 1911. According to the French biologist, Jean Lamarck, changes acquired or developed by individuals during their lifetime are transmitted to their offspring. This belief was based partly on the fact that as organs or parts of the body are used they develop and increase in strength and size. An obvious example is that of an athlete's muscles. Conversely, degeneration results from disuse, such as the loss of leg muscle mass when a person is confined to bed for an extended period. But can these bodily changes be passed to offspring? Based on simple observation the answer is "no." The children of our hypothetical athlete will not have powerful muscles unless they exercise. Another example is that despite thousands of years of circumcision male Jews and Muslims are still born with a prepuce.

Although nineteenth-century scientists believed that climate could change human physical characteristics, they considered the Jews an exception to this rule. For example, the anthropologist Johann Blumenbach was sure that geographical dispersion and various climatic conditions could not change the fundamental configuration of Jewish faces.[24] The same idea is also found in the writings of Karl Asmund Rudolph,[25] Richard Andre,[26] and Frederick Edwards.[27] The Jewish type was indelible, highly recognizable, and impervious to the influence of time and environment. Abbé Gregoire, who pleaded for emancipation of the Jews in 1789, also argued that a number of characteristics set them apart from other Europeans:

> Climate has scarcely any effect on them because their manner of life counteracts and weakens its influence. Differences in time periods and of countries have therefore often strengthened their character instead of altering their original traits. In vain their genius being fettered it has never changed, and perhaps there is more resemblance between the Jews of Ethiopia and those of England, than between the inhabitants of Picardie and those of Provence.[28]

Why were Jews assumed to be exceptions to the rules of nature? Did scientists really believe that they were different human beings to whom the laws of biology did not apply? One also wonders how many scientists subvert the nature of scientific inquiry to support their prejudices.

Other scientists were better observers. According to them the Jews physically resemble the people among whom they live. Yet, because they were sure that Jews married only Jews, they asked: "What else but the influence of climate could account for the variations in their skin color and their other physical similarity to the native population?"[29] The way the question is put, the answer can only be "nothing else." But, why did they believe that no intermingling with the "native" populations took place. After all, human beings have always intermingled. Are the Jews different from non-Jews in this respect? Not likely. The belief that Jews do not breed with non-Jews prevented scientists from discovering the true reason for the physical similarity between Jews and their-non Jewish neighbors.

A few "scholars" in the 1850s and the 1860s turned to the new science of comparative craniometry (the measuring of skulls) in their search for a Jewish type. The technique dated from 1844, when the Swedish anatomist Andreas Retzius introduced the cephalic index to define the skull shape. The index was obtained by multiplying head width by 100 and dividing the product by head length. An index above 80 was termed brachycephalic (short skull); between 75 and 80, mesocephalic; and below 75 dolichocephalic (long skulls).

As Stephen Gould puts it:

> The mystique if science proclaims that numbers are the ultimate test of objectivity, surely we can weigh a brain without recording our social preferences.[30]

In interpreting the results of their measurements, however, race scientists showed that their objectivity was impaired by their prejudices. For example, although there is no evidence for the correlation between brain weight or skull size and intelligence, race scientists decided that lower brain weight or smaller cranial dimensions were proof of inferiority. It was no coincidence that Europeans (and most race scientists were European) had larger skulls and brains than non-Europeans. If they had found that Europeans had smaller brains, undoubtedly that would have been an indicator of superiority.

The idea that skulls of Jews were different from those of non-Jews seemed to have originated with Blumenbach (1762–1840):

> It is known that the Jewish people have been spread over the whole world for centuries on end, and have nevertheless kept a pure and a

very characteristic type; this strange fact has long worried natural-
ists and physiologists. But what is more remarkable and as yet little
known is the fact this type is clearly evident in the skulls. I have had
several opportunities of verifying this, because even laymen have
been able to recognize Jewish skulls amongst the many skulls in my
cupboards.[31]

In 1864 Carl Vogt published his *Lectures on Man*, in which he
reported that the cranial index of his sample of Jews ranged
from below 75 to above 80. Rather than conclude that Jews are
as variable in skull size as Europeans, he affirmed that there are
two types of Jews, the brachycephalic and the dolichocephalic.
Nevertheless, both are recognizable enough to distinguish them
from non-Jews. Despite the contrary evidence of his own craniometric data, Vogt could not abandon the long-held belief in
Jewish racial differences. The pathologist Rudolph Virchow
(1821–1902) wanted to determine the racial makeup of the German population and sent questionnaires to thousands of school
teachers, asking them to describe the pupils' hair and eye color.
They were told *not* to include Jewish and foreign children.[32] Why
did Virchow, a man who fought anti-Semitism and deplored the
misuse of science for political aim, exclude the Jews from his
study? Did he believe Jews were foreigners and biologically different from non-Jews?

Richard Lewontin, Steven Rose, and Leon Kamin have written
in *Not in Our Genes*:

> The questions asked by scientists, the types of explanation accepted
> as appropriate, the paradigms framed and criteria for weighing the
> evidence are all historically relative. They do not proceed with some
> abstract contemplation of the natural world as if scientists were pro-
> gramable computers who neither made love, defecated, had ene-
> mies, nor expressed political views.[33]

American scholars, at the dawn of the twentieth century, were
not immune to race science. Rather than distinguish Aryans and
Jews,[34] they differentiated Anglo-Saxons or Nordics whom they
believed to be superior from every other variety of human being
(including Jews).[35] The distinction was shared by some early
prominent eugenicists, such as Charles Davenport, head of the
station for Experimental Evolution, and Paul Popenhoe, the edi-

tor of the *Journal of Heredity*, published by the American Genetics Association. Both men made statements regarding Jews that were scientifically unfounded and racist. For example, Davenport wrote:

> There is no question, that taken as a whole, the hordes of Jews that are now coming to us from Russia and the extreme Southeast of Europe, with their intense individualism and ideals of gain at the cost of any interest, represent the opposite extreme from the Early English and the more recent Scandinavian immigration with their ideals of community life in the open country, advancement by the sweat of the brow, and the uprearing of families in the fear of God and the love of the Country.[36]

Popenhoe expressed similar fears:

> In a community of rascals, the greatest rascal might be the fittest to survive. In the slums of a modern city the Jewish type, stringently elected through centuries of ghetto life, is particularly fit to survive, although may not be the physical ideal of an anthropologist.[37]

Many physicians used their scientific position to denigrate Jews. They implied without proof that Jews were more prone to certain diseases than non-Jews and attributed these tendencies to their racial make-up. To them "racial incest" (inbreeding) was the cause of a tendency toward mental instability and predisposition to a neurotic and psychopathic condition,[38] sexual complexes,[39] and tuberculosis.[40]

There was no scientific evidence to support the notion that Jews, Slavs, and Mediterranean peoples were biologically or intellectually inferior to the Nordic peoples, but the idea triumphed with the passage of the 1924 Immigration Act, which attempted to stem the massive influx of southern and eastern Europeans to the United States.

In brief, although the Jews were not easily pigeonholed and their "racial" classification differed from one scholar to another, the basic assumption that they were a separate race was widespread throughout the nineteenth century and most of the twentieth century. The notion was also shared by Jews, including Jewish scientists who believed that to combat anti-Semitism they had to use the "unscientific" methods of Race science. This is the subject of the end of this chapter.

Part 2

> The nineteenth century saw the rise of "respectable" scientific racism and the increasing preoccupation of Jewish scientists with how to respond to the claims of mainstream science that Jews were different from and indeed inferior to non-Jews.
>
> —John M. Efron

Although race science was a pseudo-science, it bloomed from the end of the nineteenth century to the middle of the twentieth century. Most people, including the victims of racism, believed in the existence of races. Jewish scholars, instead of debunking race science, practiced it to refute claims of their alleged "racial'-'inferiority.[41] Any attempt to attribute either positive or negative characteristics to humans on the basis of their physical appearance is unscientific.[42] No biological link has ever been found between psychological and physical characteristics. None has ever been found between skin color and intelligence, just as none has ever been found between the color of a horse and its ability to run.

It is no wonder that Jewish race scientists could find no evidence to refute the assertion that Jews are inferior to non-Jews. What Jewish anthropologists should have done was show that race science is bad science. If they had done so, they might not have stamped out anti-Semitism, but they might have helped discredit craniometry years before its practice was abandoned.

Instead Jewish anthropologists participated in a pseudo-scientific debate regarding differences between two groups of Jews, the Sephardim and the Ashkenazim. The first term is used for Spanish and Portuguese Jews and their descendants, and the second designates the Jews from Central and Eastern Europe and their descendants. Both names derive from two large populations of Jews in the Middle Ages. The one in Germany referred to that region as Ashkenaz and the one in the Iberia peninsula as Sepharad. The Sephardim spoke Ladino, a language which combined Spanish with Hebrew elements, whereas the Ashknenazim spoke Yiddish, a mixture of High German dialects and vocabulary drawn from Hebrew and Slavic languages. Both are still spoken today.

Non-Jews considered the Ashkenazim less desirable than the Sephardim, who were more culturally assimilated. The myth arose that the Sephardic Jews were physically more perfect than the Ashkenazim Jews and more like the original Jews. The myth seems to have originated with the Jewish race scientists, who apparently hoped that establishing this difference might combat anti-Semitism. If they could prove that the Jews were once a race as beautiful and as noble as the Aryan race, prejudice might decrease.[43] They failed.

Preliminary craniometric measurement of Jews seemed to indicate two distinct groups, the dolichocephalic group Sephardim and the brachycephalic Ashkenazim. The number of subjects in these studies was too small to draw any valid conclusion, however. For example, Augustin Weisbach examined only nineteen Jewish males,[44] and Julius measured only twelve skulls.[45] Although Samuel Weisenberg sampled 175 individuals, his claim that the ancient Hebrews were dolichocephalic and the Ashkenazim brachycephalic was questionable.[46] Very few examples of ancient Jewish skulls had been unearthed, and the sole study was by the physician and criminologist Cesare Lombroso, who examined only five skulls dating from about 150 CE, found in the Catacomb of St. Calixtus in Rome.[47] Furthermore, Weisenberg's measurements of Sephardim hardly differed from those of other Jews from Central Asia and the Middle East. It is highly unlikely that even a greater quantity would have supported their hypothesis that the Ashkenazim and Sephardim were significantly different.

I have pointed out that language classification led to race classification (Aryans and Semites), and this is another example of a jump from linguistics to biology. Two Jewish communities speaking different languages were assumed to be two biological groups, two races. But, just as Jews and non-Jews are not different races because one group speaks Hebrew and the other does not, neither are Sephardim and Ashkenazim.

The confusion between linguistics and biology was perpetuated by Mayer Kayserling (1829–1905), a German rabbi and historian,[48] and Maurice Fishberg (1872–1934), the famous Jewish American physician and anthropologist.[49] Both were victims of the contemporary misconception that race and language are somehow linked.

Like other race scientists, a number of Jewish anthropologists were guilty of linking physical and behavioral characteristics, of assuming that these were inherited together, and of espousing theories shown to be unfounded. For example, Joseph Jacobs (1851–1916), the first Jewish anthropologist, was a firm believer in the inheritance of acquired characteristics. He attributed the alleged craniometric differences between Sephardim and Ashkenazim to the effect of the environment and he wrote:

> in races where progress depends upon brain rather than muscle, the brain box broadens out as a natural consequence. . . . The application of all this to the case of the Jews seems obvious. If they had been forced by persecution to be mainly blacksmiths, one would not have been surprised to find their biceps larger than those of other folk, and similarly as they would have been forced to live by exercise of their brains, one should not be surprised to find the cubic capacity of their skulls larger than their neighbors.[50]

Adolph Neubauer, another Jewish anthropologist, was also a Lamarckian. He implied that the acquired capacity for clear thinking of the Sephardim was passed on to their descendants.[51] Contrary to many of his colleagues, he believed that Jews were a single type. According to him, a crucial factor in determining purity of race was fertility among members of the group. Since the Askenazim and the Sephardim interbreed have fertile offspring, they belonged to the same group of human beings. This is bad reasoning because all human beings can interbreed.

Jewish race scientists were men of their time. They believed in the concept of race and, like their non-Jewish colleagues, were certain that the Jews were a distinct race. The issue was more than academic. For example, the medical professionals were sure that Jews possessed a unique pathology, which protected them from certain contagious diseases but made them susceptible to insanity. Emil Kraepelin, author of *Psychiatre: Ein Lehrbuch,* stated it was impossible to tell which of the various influences—race, lifelong habits, climate, diet, or general health conditions—were responsible for insanity, but race was an etiological factor in the mental illness of the Jews.

As we shall see, the belief in a Jewish race thrived not only among biologists and physicians but also in literary and political circles.

4

The Final Solution:
The Ultimate Consequence
of Pseudo-Biology

To BELIEVE IN THE EXISTENCE OF HUMAN RACES AND THAT JEWS ARE a race is in itself not a crime, but this belief often leads to racism, which imputes superior and inferior traits to these races. Racism has led to the most violent crime against humanity, the Holocaust.

I. THE ROAD TO THE HOLOCAUST

At first, as the new liberated Jews struggled for emancipation, acceptance, and advancement, the newfangled hostility toward them (and the motivations behind it) appeared in social, economic and psychological forms; later on, it became racist and ultimately, in the 20th century, it assumed genocidal dimensions.

—Ronnie S. Landau
The Nazi Holocaust

By the end of the nineteenth century, erudite opinion was moving toward rejection of the race concept,[1] but the belief that Jews were a distinct race persisted among both Jews and non-Jews. This idea was reinforced by the misguided and biased work of race scientists and was broadcast widely in the writings of anti-Semitic authors and journalists, particularly in France and Germany.

The origin of literary racism is attributed to Joseph Arthur de Gobineau (1816–82),[2] who claimed that race is the key to understanding history. In his view, individuals have no free will and their "racial character" prompts them to act the way they do.

Gobineau deemed other influences to be of secondary importance. His theory of history was not only fatalistic but also racist because it included the doctrine of racial inequality, that is, higher races destined to rule and lower races destined to serve. Gobineau contrasted the Germans whom he described as tall, blond, blue-eyed, and highly creative, with the Jews, whom he imagined to be small, dark-haired, uncreative, unoriginal, and parasitic.

At the end of the nineteenth century, French literary anti-Semitism included such famous writers as Paul Bourget, Maurice Barrès, Charles Maurras, and Leon Daudet. In brilliant prose they portrayed Jews as cosmopolitan financiers, rapacious parasites, unscrupulous parvenus, intruders, and strangers, very different from "ordinary" Frenchmen.

In Germany a number of anti-Jewish works appeared in the 1870s. Some attacks were based on the traditional religious grounds, such as *Der Talmudjude*, written in 1871 by the theologian August Rohling. Other books were clearly racist. Wilhelm Marr's *The Victory of Judaism over Germanism* preached racial anti-Semitism, but it was mild when compared to the 1880 publication by Eugen Duhring, *The Jewish Question as Question of Race, Morality, and Culture with an Answer based on World History*. Duhring considered Judaism a racial religion and Jewish morality a racial morality.[3] He compared Jews to bacteria that contaminate the environment in which they live and kill their victims: in this case the German people.[4] He concluded that Jews had no right to exist at all, either among other nations or in a special country of their own, in Palestine or elsewhere.[5] His book set the tone for a large number of anti-Semitic writings which appeared at that time.[6]

The idea that Jews were a distinct race also played an important role in politics. Leaders in France, Germany, and Austria were elected in the nineteenth and twentieth century on anti-Semitic platforms which stressed that Jews were alien beings, different in nature from non-Jews, and responsible for all the problems confronting society. In 1878, decades before Hitler, Adolph Stocker founded the Christian Social Party in Germany, the first party to transfer the Jewish Question from the literary to the political domain.[7] Efforts were now made to exclude Jews from government. In 1878, Chancellor Otto von Bismark was petitioned by Bernard Forster, a high school teacher, and Liberman von Sonenberg, a military officer, to exclude Jews from all judicial and educational posts and to limit the immigration of Eastern European Jews into Germany. This petition was discussed in the Chamber of Deputies, which soon divided into two groups: the conservatives, who were mostly anti-Semitic, and the progressives, who denounced such prejudice. The debate lasted two days in November 1880, and although the majority of deputies were fundamentally anti-Semitic, nothing came of it. The Jewish question was on the back burner,[8] but it would reappear in the 1930s.

In Austria, Karl Lueger was the first politician to triumph anywhere in Europe on an explicitly anti-Semitic platform. Elected mayor of Vienna in 1897 and head of the Christian Social Party, he retained power until his death in 1910. Lueger was a role model for the young Adolph Hitler, who considered him the greatest burgermeister of all time.[9] In the anti-Semitism of Lueger and Von Schoenerer, another politician, Hitler saw a way to mobilize the masses against a single, highly visible, and vulnerable enemy.[10]

Political anti-Semitism appeared in France at the same time. In late 1881 the newspaper *Le Anti-juif* appeared. This paper was followed by *La Croix* and *Libre parole* which were the most virulently anti-Semitic newspapers of the 1890s.

In 1886 Edouard Drumond published *La France Juive*, a book whose thesis was that "Semites" had been seizing power in France since the 1789 Revolution; they were successfully subverting French traditions and culture; they were controlling the financial system and were exploiting the laboring masses. Thousands of copies were sold, which demonstrates that anti-Semitism was widespread in France and that race could be an extremely effective weapon. Drumond was elected a deputy from Algeria, where anti-Semitism was more virulent than in continental France, and eighteen other men committed to an anti-Semitic program also won elections. Among them was Maurice Barrès, a distinguished writer, who claimed that anti-Semitism offered the basis for "national union" against the alien and cosmopolitan Jews, a union that cut across the division of political classes.[11] Another deputy was Max Regis, possibly the most violent political anti-Semite in France at the time. Some years before, as mayor of Algiers, he had committed atrocities against Jews that forced his removal from office by higher authorities.[12] Regis, Barrès, and Drumond were not re-elected in 1902 because the anti-Semitic deputies failed to curtail the rights of Jews who were still considered French citizens. In 1940, with the fascist Vichy Government came the first laws that deprived Jews of their civil rights, and in many cases their life.

II. THE FINAL SOLUTION

If the international Jewish financiers in and outside Europe should succeed in plunging the nations once more unto a World War, then the result will not the bolshevization of the earth and thus the victory of Jewry, but the annihilation of the Jewish race in Europe.

—Adolph Hitler[13]

The apogee of racial anti-Semitism was reached under Hitler with the Final Solution, one of the most horrifying genocides in the world history. There have been others, of course, such as the slaughter, city after city, along the border of the Roman Empire by the Huns in the fourth century; the destruction of the New World and Australian indigenes, including the annihilation of Tasmanian aborigines; and the Armenian tragedy in 1915 and 1917, when at least half a million people were killed by the Turks.

It has been suggested that the Holocaust differed from other genocides not because of the enormous number of victims but because of the Nazi imperative to eliminate all Jews immediately. Such an imperative had no historical precedent. The horrors of the Holocaust have been described in detail in books and films, but often overlooked is the fact that Hitler and his cohorts murdered not only Jews, but also gypsies,[14] Poles, Soviet prisoners of war, fundamentalist Christians, prostitutes, homosexuals and other "deviants," political dissidents, the handicapped, and mentally ill, and even German soldiers who had been so badly wounded that it was decided they had no chance of leading a normal life. It is estimated that the total number of all victims reached 12 million.[15]

Jews were not killed by the Nazis for their religious beliefs simply, but because they descended from people whom their killers considered an inferior and evil race. They were assumed to have inherited immutable biological traits that put them beyond the pale of humanity. This was the driving force behind the genocide. Hitler did not invent racial anti-Semitism, but he turned it into a doctrine whose purpose was to destroy all Jews. He transformed conventional anti-Semitism with its metaphoric imagery of combat, into a war of annihilation directed not against foreign troops, but against defenseless civilians.

I must emphasize that the Nazis did not regard Jews as members of a religious group, since a Jew who converted to Christianity was still a Jew. Jewishness was inherited. One Jewish parent produced a half Jew; one Jewish grand parent produced a quarter Jew. Many of the Holocaust victims were chosen for death according to this criterion of their persecutors despite the fact that a substantial number were agnostics, Christians, and members of other religious affiliations. Their "crime" was to have a Jewish ancestor.[16]

Racial anti-Semitism was not specific to the Germans and is widespread throughout the Western culture. It is highly possible that it kept the American and the British governments from saving as many Jews as possible from extermination during World War II.[17] It is true that little could have been done to prevent Hitler from exterminating the Jews who were in Germany or in German-occupied territories. But the Allied governments could have saved thousands of Jews by opening the borders of the United States, England, and Palestine to those who tried to leave Europe. Instead, the United States did not even fill the emigration quotas set in 1924, and the British Foreign Office did its best to stem the flow of refugees into Palestine.

It seems that both governments found any excuse not to rescue Jews. The reasons they repeatedly invoked were put aside when other Europeans needed help. For example, the most frequent excuse, the unavailability of shipping, was a fraud. When the Allies wanted to find ships for non-military projects, they located them. In 1943, U.S. naval vessels transported 1,400 non-Jewish Polish refugees from India to the United States west coast; the U.S. State and War departments arranged to move 2,000 Spanish loyalist refugees to Mexico using military shipping. In March 1944, the British government provided troopships to carry non-Jewish refugees by the thousands from Yugoslavia to southern Italy and Egypt. At the same time, blaming the shipping shortage, it backed out of an agreement to transport 630 Jewish refugees from Spain to Casablanca.[18] However, the same month, the author, his brother, and about 500 other people, including some women and children, who had escaped from France were able to take a ship from Spain to Casablanca under the auspices of the American government.[19]

The Allies knew as early as 1942 that the Nazis were systematically exterminating the European Jews, but they did very little to save them. Was this due to anti-Semitism? We do not know for sure. However, in summer 1944, when part of Europe was already liberated, anti-Semitism in the United States strikingly showed its ugly face. The government established the first and last refugee emergency camp for Jewish refugees, Fort Oswego, a former Army base in northen New York. There were never more than a thousand people there, but the idea that refugees could be brought into the United States without regard to immigration quotas and visas brought an anti-Semitic outcry. Chairman of the House Immigration Committee, Samuel Dickstein, received many vicious letters. Here is an excerpt from one:

> Your attempt to keep that gang of refugees from Ft. Oswego in this country is just opening a wedge to get all that trash from Europe over here. The result will be an anti-Jewish riot.[20]

What is certain is that the Jews were considered a distinct race. Such a belief was often expressed in English and American newspapers and official government documents. For example, reacting to a statement in *La Société des Nations* condemning annihilation of the Jews, the *Christian Century* granted that "extermination of a *race* has seldom, if ever been, so systemically [sic] practiced on a grand scale as in the present mass murder of Polish Jews by the Nazi power" [emphasis added].[21] The Department of State was in full agreement with the British Foreign Office in regard to the refugee problem "which should not be considered as being confined to persons of a particular *race* or faith" [emphasis added].[22] William Vissert Hooft, a well-known churchman, firmly believed "that equating the genocide of the Jews with the oppression imposed on other Europeans was" a dangerous half-truth which could only serve to distract attention from

4: THE FINAL SOLUTION

the fact that no other *race* was faced with the situation of having everyone of its members . . . threatened by death in the gas chambers" [emphasis added].[23] One item on a Department of State questionnaire asked "Are you Jewish by *race* or faith?" [emphasis added].[24]

The idea that Jews were a race was also prevalent in Great Britain among Jews and non-Jews. For example, in December 1942, Lewis Namier, Bert Locker, and Blanche Dugdale, representatives of three Jewish agencies, raised the question of finding a refuge for persecuted Jews, particularly the children, with the Colonial Secretary, Oliver Stanley. He was told that "The parents would be willing to part with their children in order to safeguard the continuity of their *race*" [emphasis added].[25] At a conference in Bermuda in the spring of 1943 to discuss the refugee question, the point was made that anti-Semitic feeling in Britain was increasing. Therefore, it was preferable "in any public statement to avoid implying that refugees were necessarily Jewish. Instead refugees should be referred to by nationality rather than by *race*" [emphasis added].[26]

III. VICHY: MORE RACIAL THAN BERLIN

When this first German ordinance [against the Jews] appeared, Vichy had already repealed the Marchandau law and was busy reviewing naturalization and purging the medical and legal professions. Without any possible doubt, Vichy had begun its own antisemitic career before the first German text appeared, and without German order.
—Michael Marrus and Robert Paxton
Vichy France and the Jews

Not only did Vichy France have its own agenda against the Jews, but also this agenda was more racist than that of the Germans. The German legal definition of a Jew was:

someone who belongs or used to belong to the Jewish religion, or someone who has more than two Jewish grandparents. Any grandparent who belongs or had belonged to the Jewish religion counts as being Jewish.[27]

This was more moderate than the one adopted by the Vichy Government on October 3, 1940:

> A Jew is one who has three grandparents of the Jewish *race*, or who has two grandparents of that race, if his or her spouse is Jewish.[28] [emphasis added])

According to Richard Weisberg,

> Unlikely though it may at first seem, the Vichy authorities exceeded the Nazis in two ways:
>
> 1. Vichy explicitly included a notion of race in the statutory formula, the word is absent from the first German ordinance. . . . It indicated Vichy's early interest, independent of German pressure, in race, an interest that will be present as a dominant thread in a variety of completely autonomous Vichy legal developments from then on.
>
> 2. Vichy innovates—somewhat paradoxically, given the rhetorical invocation of race—by including a person of mixed heritage in the definition of a Jew if he or she has married a Jew. Vichy's consistent drive to include more people under the definition of a Jew than anyone was demanding of them is signaled here. Mixed marriages (German: *Mischehe*) and mixed-heritage individuals (German: *Mischlingl*) become implicated, and a person who never thought of himself or herself as Jewish now becomes subject to the law if married to a Jew.[29]

Hence, under Vichy it was possible for one brother to be a Jew, and the other not. If these brothers had two Jewish grandparents, and one brother married a non-Jew, he would be considered a non-Jew. If the brother married a Jew, that one would become a Jew. This distinction was justified according to the Vichy government because the brother whose spouse was Jewish obviously intended to return to his Jewish origins.

Although Vichy divided Frenchmen on the basis of race, it did not define the word "race" in the October 1940 law. It attempted to do so on June 2, 1941:

> 1. A Jew is: he or she, of whatever faith, who is an issue of at least three grandparents of the Jewish race, or of simply two if his or her

spouse is an issue herself/himself of two grandparents of the Jewish race.

    2. A person who belongs to the Jewish religion or who belonged to it on June 25, 1940, and who is the issue of two grandparents of the Jewish race.[30]

The race of an individual thus could be determined by the religious practices of his or her grandparents. The irrebuttable presumption was that someone who practiced the Jewish religion was a member of the Jewish race.

The definition in the June 1941 statute was broader than the one of the October 1940 law. Again, Richard Weisberg:

> The new definition of Jew girded the State against those mixed-heritage individuals who might claim non-Jewish status. While the 3 October law made such people Jewish only if they were married to a Jew, and while the German ordinance for the Occupied zone had included them only if they were practicing Jews, the 2 June statute combined these racial and religious factors by including all such people who, in fact, belong to the Jewish religion or had so belonged as of June 25, 1940. The latter cut-off cynically barred post-Occupation conversions, and even made the baptisms of newborns suspect after that date. Furthermore, early analysts of the statute, like Baudry and Ambre felt that it placed on the mixed-heritage evidence individual the *burden* of proving non-Jewishness and limited evidence of another "affiliation" to official adherence to a religion recognized by the state under the law before 9 December 1905 (effectively speaking: Protestantism or Catholicism). And the statute's definitions crudely disallowed any action taken by a Jewish parent to distance himself or herself from a child in order to protect the latter from Jewish definition. . . . The new statute explicitly rendered Jewish *both* mixed heritage marital partners, so that two people who never thought of themselves as being Jewish suddenly would become so by the mere fact of having married each other.[31]

There is no doubt that the Vichy statutes went further than the German Nazi ordinances. For example, according to the Germans, Jews who had married non-Jews were not sent to concentration camps, but, in France, they were at risk under the Vichy laws. Another example relates to children. Contrary to the interpretation of "racial" laws in Italy, Belgium, and Denmark, in

Vichy courts children born out of wedlock to Jewish mothers were considered Jewish by French courts. So were orphans who looked Jewish.[32]

The definition of a Jew differed within France and its possessions. In Algeria, which was then part of France proper, individuals were considered Jews by birth if they had three Jewish grandparents or two Jewish grandparents and a Jewish spouse. They remained Jews even if they converted to Christianity or Islam. By the same token, a person of those faiths converted to Judaism remained a non-Jew. In Morocco and Tunisia, which were French protectorates, the Vichy government exercised more political caution and took religious denomination into account when dealing with native Jews. Even a person who had four Jewish grandparents, but who converted to Islam or Christianity, was not considered a Jew. However, everyone who practiced Judaism was considered a Jew, even if he or she had only one Jewish grandparent. These definitions were applied to individuals born in Morocco and Tunisia, but not to those born elsewhere and residing there. These different rules meant that the same person could be a Jew in France and Algeria and a non-Jew in Morocco or could be a Jew in Tunisia, but not in Morocco, or vice versa.[33]

Variations in racial statutes were extremely important, because they determined in great part who lived and who died, but not entirely. Many families did not obey the "racial" laws. In order to arrest and kill as many Jews as possible, the German and French Nazis had to identify them, but they could not distinguish them from non-Jews. Consequently, Jews were ordered to declare themselves by registering and 287,962 people in France did so.[34] An unknown number of "Jews" did not and escaped deportation to the death camps. In some families, parents registered, but not their children. Some men or women registered, but their spouse did not. Because death awaited those who complied, why did so many assimilated Jews became Holocaust victims? It seems that they had an inexplicable confidence in Western culture and humanism. They kept telling themselves that the Germans and French were civilized people, so there was no reason to panic. They were dead wrong. Hitler changed his mind on many issues but never on the Jewish question. This was his obsession until his death. One night in June 1940, just after the fall of France, in a hotel room on the French Riviera, my father told one cousin that the French Jews were soon going to be treated like the German Jews. Our cousin insisted that it could not happen in France, whose motto was Liberty, Equality, and Fraternity. A few months later the motto was changed to Work, Family, and Fatherland by a government more fascist than Hitler's. The hunt had begun and survival often hinged on personal decisions to abandon Jewish identity by every means possible. I owe my life to my parents, not only biologically, but also politically. They refused to follow the dictates of the Vichy government; they were sure that to do so would mean death for the entire family. I also owe my life to numerous friends and to a large amount of luck.[35]

II
Why Jews Are Not a Race: Thoughts of a Biologist

Introduction to Part II

In the U.S. both scholars and the general public have been conditioned to viewing human races as natural and separate divisions within the human species based on visible physical differences. With the vast expansion of scientific knowledge in this century, however, it has become clear that human populations *are not unambiguous, clearly demarcated biologically* distinct groups.
—American Anthropology Association Statement on Race
Anthropology Newsletter (September 1998)

ONLY RECENTLY HAVE ANTHROPOLOGISTS ABANDONED THE IDEA OF human races, due in great part to developments in modern biology. For many years biologists could not agree on a definition of race and species,[1] and once they did, they should have realized sooner that the most important factor in race formation, complete isolation, never existed in human history. Why did it take so long? Most likely because the concept of race was so much a part of their thinking that they never questioned its meaning and reality.

Of course, there have always been a few scientists who doubted the existence of human races,[2] but they were handicapped by the biology of their time which could not provide the information needed to defend their position. For example, only in the last hundred years have we learned that the vehicle of heredity is not blood, as most racists still believe today, but genes. Only in the last fifty years have we learned the biochemical structure of genes. They are part of a large molecule identified as deoxyribonucleic acid, or DNA. Only in the last thirty years have we learned how genes work. They tap out instructions to the cells housing them and the instructions come from different chemical codes embodied in their particular segment of DNA. Only in the last few years have we decoded the whole human genome, and gene mapping of plants and animals continues.

Scientists now have a better understanding of the role of heredity and environment in the development of an organism. They know that both act in concert, not separately, as was thought for a long time. From the moment of conception until our death, we undergo a process which depends on both our genes and the environment in which we live. Consequently, each of us is unique. This should lead us to the idea that humans should be seen as individuals, not as members of some group called a "race" or "ethnic group."

If there are no human races, there cannot be a Jewish race. Anti-Semites do not believe this. Their view is based on bad history and bad science as I pointed out in Part I. In Part II, I want to develop the idea of what is a biological race and the idea that anti-Semitism rests in great part on discredited biological theories: blood inheritance, which was discarded by biologists years ago, and determinism (biological and cultural), which unfortunately still has advocates today. According to the first theory, human characteristics are transmitted through the blood. Many people who are not racist or anti-Semitic still use expressions that indicate the influence of this view. Determinism is of two kinds: biological determinism, or all human behavior is essentially determined by our genes; and cultural, or our unconscious acculturation is inescapable. Both have no scientific basis and deny freedom of the human consciousness.

Finally, I will explain something obvious, namely that our family names have very little to do with religion, something we can change or discard at will, and nothing to do with biology, something far harder or often impossible to alter. I can change my name to McLennan, I can become a Catholic or Hindu, but so far it has been impossible for me not to be bald or tall.[3]

5

The Myth of Human Races

Race is very real, but it is not biology.

—Alan Goodman[1]

AT FIRST GLANCE, THE IDEA THAT EACH HUMAN POPULATION IS CHARacterized by a unique combination of specific traits seems to make sense. It is not hard to distinguish dark-skinned Africans from Australian aborigines or dark-skinned Indians, because each group tends to have some traits in common that others do not have. For instance, Europeans tend to have light skin, straight or wavy hair, and noses of narrow to medium width. Sub-Saharan Africans tend to have dark brown or black skin, wiry hair, and so on. Another grouping of traits occurs with high frequency among East Asians, most of whom have pale-brown or slightly yellowish skin, straight black hair, and dark brown eyes. A critical analysis of human diversity around the world, however, reveals that this general "racial" view is, at best, simplistic.

First, although we can perceive several main groupings, there are millions of people who cannot be pigeonholed into them because they have a characteristic of one group and a characteristic of another group. Second, there is extreme diversity among individuals of the same group. For example, not all Africans have dark skin and not all Asians have epicanthic folds over their eyes. Third, no "racial" trait is restricted to one specific human group. In the case of skin color, many individuals in the world have dark skin. Some live in Africa, others in Australia, and still others in India. The epicanthic fold is very frequent among Asian populations, but it also occurs among some dark-skinned inhabitants of southern Africa. It also is found in some European children but disappears once they are adults. This common trait is part of our

69

human heritage and is expressed more strongly in some individuals than in others.

The most glaring problem in "race" categorization is that not all the individuals in a particular group have the combination of traits that they are supposed to have. Many dark-skinned Africans do not have thick lips, or curly hair, or a broad nose. Many Asians with epicanthic folds do not have a small nose and/or medium lips.

Precise observation leads us to discover that black eyes do not always go with dark skin or even with black hair. Light-colored eyes appear not only in Western Europeans, among whom they are common, but also sometimes among Native Americans and Africans. Blond hair along with darkly pigmented skin occurs among the aborigines of central Australia, who refer to it as tawny hair and believe that a blond native Australian is a reincarnated god who desires to pass some time on the Earth.

Hence, to associate a particular trait with another, or even several others, as is usually done in race classification, is not appropriate because there are too many exceptions. Only in a very loose way are the traits used to classify mankind into races associated with one another.[2] This is indicated by the fact that, when anthropologists draw maps of the incidence of a particular trait around the world, the distribution of any single trait is independent from any other. In other words, if you try to categorize human beings by one trait, such as skin color, certain broad divisions seem to emerge. If you add another trait, such as hair type, the divisions become blurred. The picture grows more confused with every additional trait that is mapped. Simply, traits such as skin color, hair type, and lip shape are largely independent of one another. They do not cluster to form a particular "racial" type.

Sets of physical characteristics are not inherited together. A child with one parent who has dark skin and thick wavy hair and the other who has light skin and straight hair may have any combination of these characteristics. "Racial" traits are not inherited together, but they are still inherited.

People who believe in the existence of races assume that humanity can be classified into groups according to identifiable physical characteristics. However, no one has been able to find a specific set of characteristics that can be used to distinguish one group from another without introducing layers and layers of ambiguity. Historically, the number of races has varied from four to more than forty. No matter how many groups we propose, we always find people who do not fit any one category. Racial classification is impossible because humanity is very diverse, and distinct lines of demarcation among groups do not exist.

Although physical characteristics are not transmitted as clusters from one generation to the next, we can observe a resemblance within groups. The reason is that people are more likely to marry someone near at hand, someone who speaks the same language, professes the same religion, observes the same traditions, and is likely to have similar traits. Frenchmen tend to marry Frenchmen; Americans tend to marry Americans; Jews tend to marry Jews. These intramarriages have created populations that differ from other populations in the frequencies of certain alleles (different forms of one gene). For such groupings, the word *deme* has been proposed, which is more appropriate than the word *race*.

The word *race* implies far greater biological distinctions than can be observed among humans. It also gives the idea that human populations are static, when really they are dynamic, continuously varying in genetic diversity. For example, although Jews are not members of a distinct race, Jewish populations are constantly changing in the frequency of certain alleles under the influence of proselytism and intermarriage.

What then are races? How are races formed?

Race formation is a step toward species formation. The splitting of one population into two smaller groups that become two species is a gradual process. It is impossible to tell at a glance when populations become races and when races cease to be races and become species. But, we can distinguish three stages.

First, race formation begins when the frequency of certain forms of a gene (alleles) differs slightly in one part of the population from the other part.

Second, if the differentiation proceeds unimpeded, most or all the individuals of one part of the population may, due to the process of mutation and selection, come to possess certain alleles which members of the other part of the population do not. We are now dealing with distinct races.

Third, biological changes that prevent the interbreeding of races may develop which splits the former single group into two or more separate ones. Once interbreeding is not possible, we are dealing with separate species.

Among humans race formation has never gone further than the first stage.

However, breeds of dogs represent stage 2, and are excellent example of what biological races are. No one has a problem differentiating them. They range from the dainty little Chihuahua to the giant St. Bernard, from the curly Poodle to the Great Dane. How did these different breeds of dogs come into existence? They have been produced by us from some earlier form by selection of desired characteristics and restricted breeding. They would not have come into existence without our intervention, and if dogs were free to breed at will, they would eventually return to the original dog.

Race is a biological term with a definite meaning. A race occurs when a population becomes sexually isolated long enough to posses exclusive alleles, and this has never happened among humans. Yet the term *race* is used every day. In the public mind this leads to great confusion, especially when social, political, and religious views are added. The result is that superficial differences are seen as inheritable and unchangeable.

Most of the distinctions among human groups are cultural. People of different national origin adhere to different religions, have different political views, and speak different languages. All these can be modified as is done every day by adopting another country, changing religion or political views, and learning another language. In the case of the Jews, to consider them a race is to equate race and religion. Jews are a religious body, not a separate biological human group. The history of the Jews that I summarize in part III reveals that they have always interbred with non-Jews and that many non-Jews have become Jews. The conditions for race formation never arose. What Jews have preserved and transmitted is a rich body of religious and cultural traditions and modes of conduct. The only valid criterion for determining membership in the group is confessional (adherence to the Jewish faith).

Later, I will write about black Jews, brown Jews, and white Jews. This classification parallels the well-known but ambiguous race classification of mankind based mostly on skin color: Does the difference in skin color justify putting people in different categories? No, for we know enough about the biology of skin color to be certain it is a matter of degree not absoluteness.

Skin color depends mostly on the amount of a pigment, called melanin, in our skin. Except for albinos, all of us have some melanin, although some populations have more pigments than others. The amount of melanin varies tremendously among individuals regardless of their group. It even varies widely among members of the same family. This leads us to the idea skin color is inherited, but its genetics are not known,[3] possibly because of the biological complexity of skin color. Differences in skin color are primarily due to the amount of melanin present in the epidermal (upper) layer of our skin. The pigment is synthesized in specialized cells, called melanocytes. Within these cells are even smaller structures, called melanosomes, in which melanin is produced.

Regardless of how dark or how light our skin appears, we all have the same skin structure, produce the same type of melanin, and have the same number of melanocytes. Differences seem to be due only to the amount of melanin, which develops in four stages. A light-skinned person has very few melanosomes in any stage of development and they occur in small units, unless their skin is exposed to sunlight for prolonged periods. People with very dark skin have a large number of melanocytes filled, with melanin and their melanosomes occuring as large single units.[4]

For many years, anthropologists believed that fair skin among the inhabitants of northeastern Europe was a long-term adaptation to cloudy skies and a cool climate with little ultraviolet (UV) radiation. A decrease in the amount of melanin permitted ultraviolet radiation to reach the inner skin and synthesize vitamin D, which is essential for proper calcium metabolism. This hypothesis, which was a good example of natural selection in humans, might be replaced by a very different hypothesis, which presumes that dark skin evolved to protect the body from losing Vitamin B folate. In a critical paper, Richard Branda and John Eaton showed that light-skinned people exposed to simulated strong sunlight had abnormally low levels of the essential vitamin B folate in their blood.[5] The significance of these findings to reproduction and, hence, evolution became clear when it was learned that vitamin B folate is essential to the synthesis of DNA in dividing cells. Anything that involves rapid cell proliferation, such as the production of sperm cells (spermatogenesis) requires vitamin B folate. This was shown in rats. It was recently reported that folic acid treatment can boost the sperm count of men with fertility problems.[6] Such observations led to the hypothesis that dark skin evolved to protect the body's folate from destruction by too much ultraviolet radiation. In northern Europe where there is far less UV radiation light skin would not be selected out.

In brief, scientists spent decades trying to establish an unambiguous race classification for human beings. In the process they demonstrated, often by accident, that any criteria were of no significance or value. The differences we share are a matter of degree and vary from individual to individual; they are not absolute. This is true even of that most obvious difference, skin color, which has played such a devastating role in shaping human relations. Scientists also have learned that there is more individual diversity among individuals than diversity among groups.

Although anthropologists began to deny the idea of race as early as in the 1960s,[7] the idea has gained wide acceptance with anthropologists only in the last twenty years. The public at large seems unaware of this shift. The terms "race" and " racial" still appear in newspapers, magazines, and political speeches, and are still used on census forms. It is still a hot topic in all sorts of public arenas ranging from college admissions and programs of affirmative action to legal rulings and medicine.

6
Jewish Blood, Genes, and Diseases: Bad Ideas

A good number of Scots must have Jewish blood in their veins, which is the reason why so many of them in that part of the Island have such remarkable aversion to pork and black puddings to this day.

—John Toland

IN THE PRECEDING CHAPTER WE HAVE SEEN THAT ONE ASSUMPTION OF race thinking, that humanity can be without ambiguity classified into groups using identifiable physical characteristics, is false. A second assumption, that these characteristics are transmitted "through the blood," is also false.

For centuries people believed that blood transmitted physical and behavioral traits to one's descendants. But "blood has nothing to do with heredity, either biologically, sociologically, or in any another matter."[1] The transmitters, as we have known since the beginning of the twentieth century, are the genes which are present in all the body cells, including reproductive cells, of every individual. Furthermore, modern science has demonstrated that not one drop of blood passes from the mother to the child. Small molecules in her bloodstream, such as antibodies and antigens, enter the fetus through the placenta, but these have no effect on heredity.

Before the birth of genetics, it was thought that the bloods of the parents combined in the blood of their child. In an isolated population this would result in a homogeneous liquid, the blood of a race, which led to such terms as blue blood, royal blood, pure blood, mixed blood, half-blood, Negro blood, and Jewish blood. Although the theory was discarded years ago, we still use these ex-

75

pressions, and the word *blood* continues to signify descent from
a common ancestor.

The belief in blood inheritance had very harmful consequences. According to the "one drop" rule, we all carry a little
tiny bit of blood from every ancestor. If an ancestor is considered
inferior in any respect, that blood taints all the descendants. This
concept was the basis for "certificates of purity" in Spain, a guarantee that their bearers had no Jewish or Moorish ancestry, and
it was the criterion the Nazis used to determine who was sent to
death camps.

Some contemporary writers, in an attempt be more scientifically literate, refer to "Jewish genes" instead of "Jewish blood,"[2]
but there is no such thing. If Jewish genes existed, they would
code for Jewish traits, but there are none.

The stereotypical physical traits assigned to Jews are small to
middling stature, a long hooked nose, oily skin, dark complexion,
black and often wavy hair, thick lips, and flat feet, plus a tendency
for women to become fat. Are these Jewish characteristics? Of
course not. Many non-Jews look that way, and many Jews do not.
For example, the so-called Jewish nose is hardly more frequent
among the Jews than a pug nose,[3] and it appears very frequently
among non-Jews in the Middle East, among the Scots, and in the
mountains of Germany. Many non-Jews have flat feet, and the
majority of fat women are not Jewish. The lip shape of Jews and
the color and the type of hair do not differ from those that occur
in the rest of the population. To be biologically different, Jews
would have to have genes that non-Jews do not possess, and so
far scientists have not been able to find any.

This leads us to another erroneous concept. A person often
claims to have various proportions of ancestral stock, such as
one-quarter English or one-sixteenth Italian. This usage dates
back at least to the Middle Ages, when someone with only a
thirty-second part of Jewish ancestry was considered a Jew. All
such references to a fraction of ethnic origin have no meaning
genetically for two reasons. First, if ethnic or racial chromosomes existed (which I must emphasize is not true), the hereditary relationship of "mixed" descendants to any ancestral group
would depend entirely on the number of chromosomes of that
group they carry. But it can be shown biologically that it is impossible to determine what such a number might be.[4] For exam-

ple, if a man who has a Jewish father and a non-Jewish mother marries a non-Jewish woman, all his children will be considered socially one-fourth Jewish. Each female child is assumed to receive from this Jewish grandfather one-quarter of his chromosomes, in actuality each could carry any proportion, from zero to twenty-three of the supposed "Jewish" chromosomes. The proportion for a male child is slightly different because each male receives a Y chromosome from his father. Hence, it is possible for a person who is socially considered one-sixteenth Jewish to carry more supposed "Jewish" chromosomes than a female who is considered one-eighth or even one-fourth Jewish.

Second, references to ethnic stock have no meaning genetically because there are no national genes. Such terms as French, Irish, and German refer to nationalities. The term Jewish refers to a religion, not genes.

In summary, there are no Jewish, Christian, or other blood lines. Blood does not transmit heredity, and no drop of blood passes from mother to child. There are no Jewish genes because Jews do not have unique traits. It is interesting to note that numerous writers object to the expression "Jewish blood."[5] But, I have found none who object to the expression "Jewish genes." Both terms should be rejected, as should the notion of Jewish diseases.

A colleague of mine does not agree that there is no such thing as a Jewish race. She insists that Jews are biologically different because they have diseases that non-Jews do not have. This is not correct. What is true is that some rare hereditary diseases are less rare among some Jews than among non-Jews. The incidence of these diseases varies markedly between groups of Jews, however. It is also true that some hereditary diseases are less rare among non-Jews than among Jews.[6]

Tay-Sachs disease, also called infantile idiocy, is the best example of a hereditary disease which predominantly affects one group of Jews, the Ashkenazim. The disease causes degeneration of cerebral function soon after birth due to an accumulation of lipids in the cytoplasm of neurons in the brain. Death usually occurs during the first or second year of life. The incidence of this disease is presented as evidence that Jews are genetically distinct from non-Jews, because the frequency of the Tay-Sachs gene among non-Jews is 100 times less than among the Ashkenazi Jews. But recent research has shown that the frequency of the gene is astonishingly even less among Sephardic and Oriental Jews.[7] Should we agree with my colleague that the Sephardim and Ashkenazim are two different races of Jews? What about the Moroccan Jews and the French Canadians among whom many cases of Tay-Sachs disease were recently found?[8] Do they belong to one race or two?

Tay-Sachs among Moroccan Jews is due to a mutation different from the one that causes the disease among Ashkenazi Jews. As to the French Canadian mutation, it may be unique to a lineage with a counterpart in France. An examination of parish and civil records for the clusters of the French Canadian families in southeast Quebec and northeast Brunswick might help to determine its origin..

A well known human geneticist, Victor A. McKusick, writes:

Studies of special populations have taught us much about population genetics in general: I refer to the Finns and the Amish, for example, in addition to the Jewish populations. Although particular disorders may be usually frequent (or rare) in such populations, the lessons learned from their study are generally applicable because mutation is no respecter of the individual—usually it turns out that these disorders occur in all people. The principles illustrated by example in Jewish and other distinct populations, or deduced from their study apply to all populations. The clinical, biochemical, and genetic characteristics of their diseases are found, even when the patients are of quite different ethnic extraction.[9]

In conclusion, there is no Jewish blood: there are no Jewish genes; there are no Jewish diseases.[10]

7

The Jews: Victims of Determinism

I. BIOLOGICAL DETERMINISM

It is interesting to speculate what amount of financial ability
he owed to his ancestor, Sampson Gideon Abudiente, the famous "Jew broker" of his age.

—Cecil Roth

THE ABOVE STATEMENT REFERS TO H. C. E. CHILDERS, WHO BECAME
Chancellor of the Exchequer under British Prime Minister Glad-
stone. One of his ancestors, Sampson Gideon Abudiente, was
born into a converso family that settled in England after expulsion from Spain. Abudiente was remembered not only for his
wealth but also for maintaining the financial stability of the Trea-
sury during the Jacobite Rebellion in 1745. In suggesting that
Childers inherited financial ability from his Jewish forebear,
Cecil Roth implies that this characteristic not only is hereditary,
but also is more prevalent among Jews than non-Jews. He seems
to agree with anti-Semitic propaganda that regards financial
ability (mixed with dishonesty) as a "Jewish trait," passed from
one generation to the next.

Even if we assume that financial skills are hereditary, Cecil
Roth's speculation is on shaky grounds. Childers had other ancestors, and the likelihood that Abudiente transmitted to his
great-grandson a specific characteristic is very small. Roth also
did not consider the fact that the Childers family was wealthy and
that it is very likely that the senior Childers had trained his son
to manage money.

The idea that genes expressed themselves regardless of the
environment in which a person develops is part of an old view of

heredity, which has received the name of biological determinism.[1] It wrongly assumes that heredity alone shapes us and er-
roneously equates heritable with unchangeable. Because anti-
Semites are firm believers in biological determinism, it is very
important to explain why they are wrong in believing that Jews
are helpless victims of their genes.

A human being results from the union of the mother's egg with
one of the father's sperm. The fertilized egg develops into an
adult by multiplication of its cells, which become specialized tis-
sues. Although we receive our inheritance (our genes) from our
parents, what we become also depends on the type of our environment that affects us before and after birth. Certain develop-
mental tendencies are inherent in the fertilized egg, but they are
manifested in and influenced by the environment in which the
organism develops.

> Both heredity and environment are needed. For example, if hen's
> and duck's eggs are raised in the same incubator (same environ-
> ment), they will produce respectively chicks and ducklings. On the
> other hand, if either of them were thrown into the sea, they would fail
> to produce any little birds at all. The first example demonstrates how
> important heredity is. The second demonstrates how important envi-
> ronment is.[2]

Obviously, one cannot say that heredity is more or less important than the environment since both are essential to the development of any organism. This view took a long time to be
accepted by scientists and seems not yet to have reached many
in the public at large. For example, when the world press learned
in 1996 about the cloning of the ewe, Dolly, it reported that the
baby sheep was identical to Dolly. This is not true for two reasons. First, the cell that gave rise to the baby was from the mam-
mary gland; in theory every body cell has the same DNA, but in
reality the DNA of any cell can mutate and this could have happened to the cell in question.[3] Second, even if two cells have identical DNA, they will not result in identical individuals, because
the environment in which they develop is different.

Every individual organism is the unique product of the interaction between genes and environment at every stage of life. This
is particularly true for human behavior. For many years biolo-

gists and psychologists differed on the determinants of behavior. The former emphasizes the role of heredity; the psychologist stresses the role of the environment. The confused layperson often believes in a sharp division between hereditary and environmental traits, which gives rise to certain myths. For example, hereditary disease is untreatable; an environmentally contracted disease is treatable. Or the IQ of a child depends on schooling, so intelligence cannot be hereditary. Or because intelligence is hereditary, a person's IQ score remains the same throughout life.[4] In fact, a genetic disease such as diabetes can be treated and controlled with insulin; people vary in intelligence, but their results on IQ tests are related to their academic achievement.

The division of traits into strictly hereditary and environmental categories is untenable, because any trait has a genetic and an environmental component. It can be modified by changes in the genes and by manipulation of the environment. Hence, the genetic component in intelligence need not hinder us from educating our children. Except for a pathological minority, all humans respond to some extent to education; however, we should be aware of the inborn genetic diversity among students who need different approaches of learning to profit as much as possible from schooling.

Biological determinism, I repeat, claims that genes determine human behavior regardless of the environment in which we are raised. If determinists are right, we should be able to predict the behavior of someone if we know the nature of his or her genes. Thus far there is no proof that this is possible, but that does not prevent the most extravagant claims of determinism regarding the Jews. They are said to be a nomadic people, due to some inherited trait that persists despite environmental change (economic, social, or political). In other words, they move not because they are persecuted or expelled, but because of this biological imperative.

During the 1970s a new discipline was formed, sociobiology, which claims there are genes for aggression and territoriality. This supposedly explains the existence of violence in society, as well as racism and sexism. In other words, it offers a genetic, and therefore determinist, explanation for social difference and the continued domination of one group by another.

Let us return for a moment to the ewe, Dolly. I noted that she and her clone were quite similar but not identical because of possible differences in DNA and their environment. What is true for sheep is also true for human beings. Identical twins who are reared in unrelated families are very similar, but not exactly the same in appearance or behavior. From time to time striking examples of similarities between long-separated twins are reported in the press, but scientific analysis of such data finds that these cases are very rare. The public is not made aware of this because examples to the contrary are not newsworthy and go unreported. Indeed, studies of separated twins leads us to believe that environment plays a role in molding behavior. Therefore, children of Jewish parents adopted by non-Jews very early in life will probably behave differently than raised in a Jewish environment. It is very likely that they will not consider themselves Jews and will not be considered so by non-Jews.

Despite its unscientific basis, biological determinism continues to shape the thinking of racists, anti-feminists, and others who want to believe in a biological heritage that transcends individual experience and choice. To presuppose that we have no freedom to think for ourselves, choose, and change, is to deny our humanity.

II. Cultural Determinism

> Culture is wholly acquired by learning and imitation, and transmitted entirely by teaching and precept.
> —Theodosius Dobzansky

Cultural determinism is a "doctrine that assumes that our cultural heritage passed down by a process of unconscious acculturation is inescapable."[5] This is the case with Judaism, which is culturally inherited, but often thought to be biologically inherited.

When Jean-Marie Lustiger became a French cardinal in 1986, he said to a reporter of *Time* magazine:

> I have always considered myself a Jew, even if that is not the opinion of some rabbis. I was born Jewish and so I remain, even if that is not acceptable to many" [emphasis added].[6]

Why did he believe he was born Jewish? Cardinal Lustiger was born in France, where his parents settled after leaving Poland

and became French citizens. They foresaw the need to protect their son from Nazi persecution of the Jews after the German invasion of France in June 1940 and in August they had him baptized as a Catholic in Orléans, at the age of 13. The future cardinal changed his name from Aaron to Jean-Marie and joined a monastery. Several years later he became a priest, and climbed the ranks of the Catholic hierarchy.

In saying that he was born a Jew, Cardinal Lustiger, like many people, confuses two types of inheritance, biological and cultural. Other animals have only the first, but humans have created the second. We pass on to our children not only our genes, but also our specific culture, which E. B. Tylor defines as a complex whole that includes knowledge, belief, art, morals, law, customs, and any other capabilities and habits acquired by us as members of society.[7] The key word is "acquire," because culture is not biologically transmitted.[8] It must be taught to us by previous generations, whether grandparents, parents, or other human beings, by imitation, training, learning, and thinking.

To be sure, environment and heredity can make the acquisition and transmission of culture, or some of its aspects, easier or more difficult. For example, some of us are more skillful than others in understanding, speaking, or writing languages. Nevertheless, all healthy individuals have the capacity to learn and speak at least one language. This, like the capacity to walk erect, if I am permitted to say, is in our genes.[9] A crucial point, however, is that biological heredity does not determine which language a person will use. That is in great part influenced by the child's parents. I remember meeting in Venezuela a little girl not yet three years old who talked to me in Spanish a mile a minute. Had she lived elsewhere, she would have mastered English, French, German, or whatever.

Just as there are no genes for speaking a specific language, there are no genes for practicing a specific religion. That also is strongly influenced by parentage. In other words, the characteristics a human being acquires during his or her lifetime are not transmitted to offspring biologically, but culturally. Among these are not only language and religion, but also patterns of behavior, reasoning, and social attitudes. We are taught these from infancy, and we take them so completely for granted that we become aware of them only when confronted with people who have acquired different ones.

We are the product of both, our biological and our cultural inheritance. It is hard to distinguish the contributions of each. In some cases, however, children do not inherit the culture of their parents, most notably because of adoption. For example, when American couples have adopted Asian children, the child may not resemble them physically, but will be American, will speak English, eat turkey at Thanksgiving, celebrate the Fourth of July, and most likely receive toys at Christmas. And if their adoptive parents are religious, they will follow them to their place of worship.

A less striking case of biological and cultural inheritance separation is American children born from immigrants who generally behave very much like any other American child. They have not biologically inherited the "behavioral traits" of their parents and ancestors. Instead, they acquire behavior common to American children, such as putting catsup on French fries and turning their caps backward.

Years ago, the late geneticist, Theodosius Dobzhansky, commented: "Since culture is acquired by training, people are not born but learn to be American, Chinese, or Hottentot."[10] We can extend this to the idea that people are not born but learn to be Christian, Muslim, or Jew. That is why Cardinal Lustiger should have said: "I was born in a Jewish family," or, "my ancestors were Jewish." That is also why I have also a problem with the expressions "half a Jew" or "half Jewish." Scott Simon, the PBS newscaster, once described himself in this manner and I know what he meant, of course: one parent was Jewish. Nevertheless the term should be discarded because it suggests biological inheritance. I am tempted to ask Scott Simon which half is Jewish. "Up to his waist" was the answer that Groucho Marx came up with when asked whether his "half-Jewish" son could go into a pool from which Jews were restricted.[11] I also would like to ask Scott Simon what constitutes his other half, Catholic, Protestant, or Hindu?

A child from a Jew and a non-Jew cannot be compared to the fictitious Mr. Spock, second officer of the Starship *Enterprise* or *Star Trek*, who supposedly had a Vulcan father and an Earthling mother. Spock had pointed ears like his father and a heart on the left side like his mother. We could say that he is half Vulcan and half Earthling, because he inherited characteristics specific to two different biological beings. We cannot say that someone is half-Jew and half-Catholic, however, because the parents are not two different biological beings, and their children do not inherit biological traits specific to a Catholic or to a Jew. Judaism and Catholicism are religions of which one may be a member of either, but not half a member of both.

I believe that the expressions "born a Jew"[12] and "half a Jew" are relics of fallacious blood theory of inheritance. They indicate that many of us still believe consciously or unconsciously in the erroneous concept that Jews are a distinctive race.

III. JEWISH NAMES AND BIOLOGY

Liberty is not to keep a [family] name if one wants to, it is to change if one desires.
—Fernand Corcos, *Auto-reform*

I have a friend named Robert Isay. Most people assume that he is Jewish, because "Isay" is a "Jewish" name. But he is not, nor is his wife, his mother, or his grandmother. This family name comes from his father, who got it from his own father, who may have been Jewish. I have another friend named Jack Cohen. He obtained the family name from his father, but in a different manner: he was adopted by the Cohen family when he was three months old.

Family names are socially, not biologically inherited. In many parts of this male-dominated world, the family name is transmitted from the father to his children. Sons keep that name, but a daughter generally takes the name of her husband. Even if she does not, her children will have their father's name. Whatever the naming custom followed, it is the social practice of a given culture. Furthermore, many societies permit name changes.

For example, in Great Britain during World War I, hundreds of Jewish families with German names anglicized them in order to avoid suspicion of loyalty.[13] In Europe during World War II, many individuals with "Jewish" names "aryanized" them in order to escape death. In order to escape anti-Semitism in the United

States, many Americans of Jewish extraction changed their names.[14]

From a biological point of view, the transmission of family names through the male line makes little sense. It ignores the female genetic contribution, which in fact is more important than the male's. Let me explain. Every cell in our body is roughly made up of two parts, the nucleus and the cytoplasm. Both contain DNA, the material that makes up the genes. The genes in the nucleus are carried in the chromosomes and the genes in the cytoplasm are carried in specialized organelles, the mitochondria. It has long been known that each parent contributes the same amount of nuclear genes to their offspring, but all the mitochondrial genes are of maternal origin contributed by the egg cytoplasm.[15] Sperm have few mitochondria, which furnish the energy needed for the sperm to reach their destination. These mitochondria are lost in the process of fertilization.

Furthermore, virtually everything a mother does during gestation has an effect on fetus development, and sometimes this kind of nurture continues after birth because of breast feeding. It is more logical from a biological point of view that women transmit the family name. Even from a social perspective this should be the case among Orthodox Jews, who insist that to be a Jew one must have a Jewish mother.

Due to naming customs, adoption, and freedom of choice, a person with a Jewish name may not be Jewish,[16] and a person with a non-Jewish name may be Jewish. Despite this, anti-Semites believe that anyone with a Jewish name is automatically Jewish. Raphael Alibert, the French minister of Justice in the Vichy regime, wanted to be sure that no lawyer of the "Jewish race" escaped persecution. He instructed the police to look for both first and family names that were Jewish and then find out whether such people had ancestors buried in Jewish cemeteries.[17]

Anti-Semites are not the only ones who believe that a Jewish name indicates that someone is a Jew. For example, Fernand Corcos, my uncle and an opponent of anti-Semitism, cites the names of twenty-one Nobel Prize winners and tells us that they are Jews or half-Jews.[18] I knew him well and I had much respect for him, but I wonder where he obtained his information. Was it from their names alone? In fact some of these people did not practice Judaism, and he does not list others who were practicing Jews but did not have "Jewish" names.

Incidentally, I do not believe that citing famous Jewish scientists and artists helps in any way to fight anti-Semitism. Is there anything in the biological nature of Jews that ensures success or talent? My uncle was not entirely clear on this subject. He seems to believe that their achievement was due to a contribution of hard work and intelligence, but this is also true for non-Jewish Nobel laureates. It is more likely that Jews, like Asian Americans, were and are still pushed to excel in schools.

In brief, family names are a social convenience. They tell us nothing about the biological nature of individuals, their background, what they believe, and what they think.

III

Why Jews Are Not a Race: A Short History of the Jews

Introduction to Part III

Proximity provides the opportunity for intermarriage, and intermarriage is the means by which genetic exchanges occur.

—Harry Shapiro
Race and Science

MODERN BIOLOGY TEACHES US THAT IN ORDER FOR A POPULATION OF organisms to become a distinct race, the population must be sexually isolated for a long time. Therefore, in order for Jews to be a distinct race of human beings, they would need to have been isolated from non-Jews for many generations, but this was never the case. Throughout their entire history Jews mated with non-Jews and absorbed many people who converted to Judaism. In fact, there have been periods when this proselytism and mating were intensive. The Jews also have experienced other events that counter genetic isolation: immigration, emigration, slavery, adoption, rape, and promiscuity.

Intermarriage by Jews and non-Jews has generally been ignored by historians,[1] but from a biological point of view the fact should be stressed. It has very important consequences for the anti-Semitic belief that Jews are biologically different from others. If the offspring of these marriages are raised as Jews and marry Jews, then non-Jewish elements, if they exist, are incorporated into the Jewish people. If the children are not raised as Jews and marry non-Jews, then Jewish elements, if they exist, are incorporated into the non-Jewish population. In both cases any unique biological differences that may have existed disappeared long ago. The Nazi racial laws and the final solution came too late to prevent the "Aryan race" from being contaminated by "Jewish blood." The harm was already done.

Religious conversion is another way to mingle populations. Although conversion to Judaism is less frequent today than in the past, it has been common throughout history. Even more com-

91

mon is forced conversion to Christianity, imposed on Jews, as a group, under the threat of expulsion or death. Jewish children were sometimes kidnaped and forcibly baptized. As a result a large number of non-Jews, including anti-Semites, have Jewish ancestors.

In this part of the book, I present evidence that the Jews continually received an inflow of genes from neighboring populations as a result of conversion and intermarriage. This flow is greatly underestimated because when matings occurred outside marriages, especially in the case of rape, there are no records and the exact number of offspring of these matings is unknown. Furthermore, interfaith marriages between Jews and non-Jews are underestimated in many countries over the last two hundred years, because the religion of the newlyweds is not recorded in civil ceremonies. Cases of conversion are also underestimated because little attention is paid, unless individuals are celebrities. The history of the Jews reveals that they were never sexually isolated and, therefore, could not be a distinct biological race.

8
In the Beginning

Neither shalt thou make marriage with them; thy daughter thou shalt not give unto his son, nor his daughter shalt thou take unto thy son.

— Deuteronomy 7:13

IF JEWS HAD FOLLOWED THE ABOVE COMMANDMENT FOR GENERA-tions, they might have developed characteristics which could justify their classification as a distinct race. Instead, throughout history, Jews have married non-Jews and absorbed them into their midst, so the conditions for the formation of a distinct race never arose.

Jews begin their history with Abraham.[1] According to the narrative in Genesis, Abraham was a native of Ur, a town in Chaldea. He received "a divine call" to abandon the country of his birth and settle in the land of Canaan, known today as Palestine. His offspring formed a migratory clan that settled eventually in Egypt, where they were accepted by Egyptian rulers and their population increased considerably. Then Egyptian animosity grew and the Jews were reduced to serfdom. Under the guidance of Moses, they fled and sought refuge in the wilderness of the Sinai. After a period of wandering and hardship, but united by religion, the Jews reentered Canaan around 1160 BCE and reconquered it. This is the biblical account of the Jews, who trace their lineage to a single patriarchal founder.

If nothing else, this story should convince anyone that Jews married non-Jews, and mixed with others from Day One. Many of the patriarchs had non-Jewish wives or concubines with whom they had children. Abraham cohabited with Hagar, an Egyptian, and sired Ishmael. Isaac had only one wife, his cousin Rebecca, and only two sons, Esau and Jacob. Esau married a Hittite and

Jacob married two of his cousins, Leah and Rachel; at least two of their sons married non-Jews. Judah wed the daughter of Shea, a Canaanite, and Joseph married Asenath, the daughter of an Egyptian priest. As for Moses, the hero of the Exodus, who "created" the Hebrew people, he married a Midianite and then a Cushite.[2]

Biblical accounts underestimate the matings between Jews and others for two reasons. First, marriages between Jewish women and non-Jewish men were not recorded. Wives were considered unimportant, being the property of their husbands. Second, polygamy and concubinage flourished at that time throughout the region. A man could have any number of wives so long as he supported them, but only kings and princes could afford the luxury of a large harem.[3] King David's harem included daughters of neighboring kings.[4] Among his numerous children was King Solomon, who had a large harem. Within it were many non-Jewish women, some taken in matrimonial alliances.[5] One of his wives was the daughter of the Egyptian pharaoh,[6] and another foreign wife, Naamah, bore Rehoboam, the first king of Judah.[7] It was common for a man to have at least two women in the house, a wife and a concubine (who was often a non-Jewish slave), and with both of whom he had children.[8] There is no way to determine the number of slaves in biblical Palestine, they may have constituted around 20 percent of the population.[9] Most were conquered in the numerous wars the Jews waged, and many female slaves as well as other non-Jewish women were either raped by or married to the Jewish victors and became mothers of Jews.

Opportunities for Jews to mate with others also existed in peacetime, because Palestine was so accessible to all kinds of commercial traffic between Babylonia and Egypt. Some of the travelers remained and married Jews. Their children were raised as Jews, and possibly increased the biological diversity of the Jewish population, which at that time was small.

A few years after the death of Solomon there was a historic rupture among the twelve Hebrew tribes. The ten in the North formed the Kingdom of Israel and the other two became the Kingdom of Judah. The northern Kingdom was from the beginning troubled by frequent dynastic disturbances, palace revolutions, conspiracies, and assassinations. In 721 BCE, Samar, the capital, was captured by the Assyrians. King Hoshea was taken into exile with most of his people, and they were absorbed into their foreign surroundings. The Kingdom of Judah lasted until 586 BCE, when it was destroyed by the Babylonians. Part of the Jewish population remained in Palestine, and the rest carried off to Babylon or fled to Egypt where there was still a large number of flourishing Jewish communities.

The Jews taken to Babylon were the wealthiest and most cultured. They were readily absorbed into Babylonian society and many lost their Jewish identity, especially those who married local women.[10] An unhappy minority of religious fundamentalists regarded Babylonian civilization as abominable, yearned for their homeland, and kept every custom which bound them to the past.[11] They returned to Judah fifty years after the destruction of Jerusalem, when the king of Persia, Cyrus the Great, allowed them to do so. They discovered that their coreligionists who had remained in Palestine no longer observed the orthodox religious practices and often had married non-Jewish women. Alarmed that the growing laxity would destroy the nation and its faith, they insisted on an early form of puritanism. Ezra, the zealous Babylonian royal scribe, was assisted by the governor, Nehemiah, in this reformation, which included a relentless war against intermarriage now so widespread that it was endangering the Jewish language.[12] Men who lived with non-Jewish women were to put them aside immediately under peril of ostracism. Homes were broken up; families were wrecked. The cost was high, but Ezra insisted that the end justified the means.[13] Parts of this story may reflect the imagination of pious chroniclers and Ezra himself may be a fictitious character,[14] but it is true that there was a steady reaction to religious laxity and intermarriages.[15]

Immigration and emigration played an important role in ancient times. For example, after the subjugation of the Kingdom of Israel, a major portion of the population was taken to Assyria and replaced by non-Jews from various parts of the empire. The new settlers adopted Jewish customs, helped the Jews who returned from captivity rebuild the Temple, and a few years later converted wholeheartedly to Judaism.

Conversion to Judaism was also accomplished by force. In 142 BCE, under the high priest Simon, an admirable and successful leader, the little Jewish state was again independent after centuries of servitude. The people became proud of their Judaism and successfully spread the principles of the holy writ.[16] Simon's son Hycarnus felt politically strong enough to give Israel's ancient enemies, the Edomites, only two choices: conversion, or exile.[17] During the reign of Alexander Jannaeus (103–76 BCE), several neighboring peoples were also converted to Judaism by force. They merged into the Greek-speaking Jewish society of Judah and assumed high position in the Jewish priesthood and Judean administration.[18]

By the early first century, the area of the Jewish state and its population had increased tenfold. The conditions for proselytism were highly favorable. Paganism was decaying, and sensitive minds were repelled by it. Monotheism and the seemingly rational practices of the Hebrews were expounded by the Hellenized Jewish writers and made a deep impression and great numbers converted to Judaism or followed Jewish practices and ideals. The lights of the Sabbath gleamed through the darkness from many cultured homes. Ironically, it was among those Roman citizens that the early Christians made their first converts.[19] Jewish proselytism, facilitated by the translation of the Torah into Greek in the mid third century BCE, brought more biological diversity within the Jewish population.

Despite the admonitions to remain pure, ancient Jews married non-Jews and converted others to Judaism. This explains how they came to differ in appearance. Some were tall and some were small; some had fair hair and some had black hair; some were light-skinned and some were dark-skinned.[20]

9

Jewish Proselytism

Throughout the history of the Jews, both in their land and in the diaspora, proselytes joined them individually and occasionally in groups. If we assume that the Jewish population of the biblical period constituted a race—an improbable supposition as we saw in the preceding chapter—proselytism alone would have been sufficient to destroy any "racial" unity.

I. The Roman Empire

> Anticipating the triumphant success of Christian propaganda the Jewish variety won many adherents at this period. This may lead us to think twice about the exact origins and ancestry of what came to be called the Jewish race.
>
> —Leon Poliakov
> *The History of Antisemitism*

The last chapter explored the Jewish beginnings, documenting the intensive intermarriage of Jews and conversion of non-Jews to Judaism. These same activities intensified during the Roman Empire just before the birth of Christianity. The number of Jews in the Roman Empire is estimated at 6 or 7 million,[1] or roughly 12 percent of the total population, around 50 million. This substantial proportion cannot be explained by natural increase alone, even if the Jews were very prolific. The surplus must be attributed to conversion,[2] and it is likely that converted Jews far outnumbered original Jews.[3]

It was during the Second Temple period (539 BCE–70 CE) that the Jewish faith experienced its greatest expansion. Within the Roman Empire and beyond, all kinds of people adopted completely or in part the Jewish way of life.[4] Proselytism was intense,

97

especially during the last years of the Roman Republic, as indicated in the writings of Cicero and other Romans.

Why did so many convert to Judaism? It has been argued that Roman religious creeds weakened with the spread of oriental cults that were more attractive. Among these was Judaism, which was perceived as a religion more sensitive to the needs of the poor and the abused people. The antique world ignored compassion and charity. Slaves frequently were treated far worse than animals and might be crucified by their masters or sent to the arena to be eaten by lions, or killed as gladiators. The Jews believed that slaves should have at least one day of rest during the week on the Sabbath.[5] The educated class was attracted to Judaism for its monotheism, and among the famous converts were Poppea Sabina,[6] the wife of Emperor Nero; Fluvia, the wife of a senator in the Tiberian era; Flavius Clemens, a nephew of Emperor Domitius; and the knight Emilius Valens.[7]

Judaism absorbed not only Romans but also Syrians, Arabians, and Abyssinians, as well as other Africans. Philo, a Jewish philosopher in Alexandria, wrote at the beginning of the first century CE: "Our customs are spreading and converting the barbarians and the Greeks, the East and the West, the whole earth from one end to the next." Josephus Flavius wrote in *Against Apion*: "There is no Greek or barbaric town, not one nation where the sabbath is not practiced."[8] The success of this proselytism was deplored by many Roman writers, including Dio Cassius, Juvenal, Seneca, and Tacitus. For example, Juvenal described how "Roman families degenerate into Judaism."[9] According to Seneca, the pagans embraced Judaism in great numbers, either completely or as proselytes at the gate,[10] observing one or another Jewish custom, such as the Sabbath, and their children often became full converts.

When the Jews rebelled against the Romans and were defeated by Emperor Hadrian in 134 CE, a series of decrees were issued against them. Adherence to the Jewish religion was forbidden. Circumcision, Sabbath observance, and study of the Torah were declared capital crimes. These mark the first political action to separate Jews from Christians as the latter were excluded from the decrees because they had not participated in the revolt. Until the uprising, the Romans had considered them to be Jews. The distinction between the two faiths was used by the Christians to their advantage, and Judeo-Christian evangelism intensified at the expanse of Jewish proselytism which was now punishable by death,[11] as was marriage between Jews and Christians.[12]

Nevertheless, until 391 CE, when Christianity became the official religion in the Roman Empire, the condition of the Jews had been, on the whole, indistinguishable from that of other peoples within the empire, and there were frequent intermarriages. The Roman Empire was a true melting pot during several centuries. As Leon Poliakov remarked, "this observation has a certain piquancy about it, if we think of the stubborn persistence of racial interpretations of the Jewish question by authors who are sometimes far from being anti-Semites."[13]

II. THE ARABIAN LANDS

The Jews in the Arab countries preached their religious truth to the Arabs, many of whom were familiar with the biblical tales and the epics of the Fathers. The Arabs believed that Ishmael, son of Abraham and Hagar, was the forefather of their tribes, and that the Jews were therefore blood relatives.

—Samuel Glassman
Epic of Survival

FOLLOWING THE DESTRUCTION OF THE SECOND TEMPLE BY THE Romans in 70 AD, Jews moved into Arab-controlled lands, and by the middle of the fifth century they had reached the southernmost tip of the Arabian Peninsula. Wherever they settled, they made many converts, including kings. For example, King Kariba As'ad, of Hymar, in the southwestern corner of the Arabian peninsula, converted to Judaism along with all his people in the fourth century AD.[14]

Two centuries later, a leader of the Himyarites named Dhu-Nuwas (516–25 AD) took the name of Joseph when he became a Jewish priest.[15] He resented the harsh treatment of the Jews by the emperors of the Eastern Byzantine Empire and threatened revenge on the Christians. Directly west of Yemen, in the Christian kingdom of Abyssinia, the king was urged by the emperor of

Byzantium to invade Yemen, and King Joseph was defeated and committed suicide. Many of his Jewish subjects then converted to Christianity and later to Islam. Those who did not were forced to move to Palestine or Iraq.[16]

Also during the late Second Temple period in the ancient kingdom of Parthia, northeast of present-day Iran, the royal house of Adiabene adopted the Jewish faith, and proved to be its zealous defenders.[17] Whereas the royal family made the choice freely, slaves were converted by force. One historian estimated that the slave conversion in the Arab lands doubled the number of Jews there.[18]

In pre-Islamic Arabia not only was conversion from one religion to another frequent, but so was marriage between Jews and Arabs. The most famous example concerned the prophet Muhammad, who married Safiyya, the daughter of a Jew, and who had at least one Jewish concubine, Raybna. Jews also married among peoples drawn into the Muslim orbit by the Arab conquests, despite the best efforts of both Muslim and Jewish authorities to discourage sexual relations between those of each faith.

Conversion to Judaism decreased considerably when the Arabs established the Muslim Empire in which any religion but Islam was prohibited. Nevertheless, Jewish communities survived in Arabia through thirteen centuries of harsh and oppressive Muslim rule. The most important group is the Yemenite Jews, who are mostly the descendants of Arabs who converted to Judaism in pre-Islamic times. Today, many of them live in Israel, where they contribute their share of human diversity.

III. Africa

Proselytism played an important role in North Africa, where Jews may have helped the Phoenicians found trading posts.[19] The Phoenicians responded positively to Judaism because they tended to believe in only one god and circumcision was an established practice among them. They adopted many of the Jewish rituals, such as lighting candles for the Sabbath,[20] and their customs likely would have spread among the local populations as their trading posts grew into towns and cities.

Because of similarities in beliefs, language,[21] and experience,[22] it is likely that the Phoenicians swelled the ranks of Jewish converts after the fall of Carthage (146 BCE), which would explain their puzzling disappearance during the first centuries of the Christian era.

According to the historian Josephus Flavius, there were 500,000 Jews in Cyrenaica (part of modern Libya) in the first century of the Christian era. Only conversion can explain such a large number, and historical documentation attests that it occurred.[23] However, the figure Flavius cites may not be trustworthy, because in 76 BCE Cyrenaica was annexed to the Roman Empire, and the Berber lands were seized and given to Roman colonists. The Berbers joined forces with the Jews, who were also persecuted by the Romans and both fought Rome for many years. Eventually they were defeated and took refuge in lands close to the Sahara which today are within Tunisia and Algeria.

One of these Judeo-Berber communities, Touat,[24] flourished until 1492 when it was overrun by Muslim fanatics. We now associate the Berbers with Islam, but before the Arab conquest reached North Africa, the Touat was a major center of Judaism.[25] Gravestones engraved with Hebrew characters have been found at Camara.[26] An inscription on a lead tablet dating from the Roman period, discovered in the metropolis of Hadrumetum, invokes the God of Abraham, Isaac, and Jacob. Similar proof is found among Punitic antiquities.[27] Tertian reports that the Berbers observed the Sabbath as well as Jewish festivals, feasts, and dietary laws.[28]

Historians suggest that the Berbers converted to Judaism because they were influenced by the Carthagenian civilization, which espoused a monotheistic religion[29] and a moral code similar to that of the Jews.[30] Many Jews of North Africa are believed to descend from Berbers who were converted to Judaism in the third century.[31] Their unorthodox Judaism is a mixture of Jewish, Berber, and Carthagenian customs.

Jewish proselytism declined sharply after 325 CE, when the Council of Nicea made reforms that helped unify the Christian Church and aided the spread of Christianity. Religious changes in North Africa followed a familiar pattern: from paganism to Judaism, to Christianity, to Islam. The religious history of these populations demonstrates the futility of genetically distinguishing a Jew from a Christian or a Christian from a Muslim.

Elsewhere in Africa, the Jews also made converts. An interesting and controversial case is the Falashas of Ethiopia. These dark-skinned people could not be distinguished from their neighbors by their dress or physical appearance.[32] They grew the same crops, raised the same cattle and farmed the same land. What made them different from their neighbors was that they practiced for centuries a pre-rabbinic form of Judaism.

Only recently have Jews outside Ethiopia acknowledged that the Falashas are indeed Jewish.[33] Why this long delay? According to the traditional view all Jews originated in Palestine and were dispersed over the earth as a result of Assyrian, Babylonian, and Roman conquests. Dark-skinned people did not fit this picture. The idea that the Falashas had been converted to Judaism at some time in the remote past finally became acceptable to Jewish historians. If Christianity, Buddhism, and Islam had spread by extensive conversion, and not simply by migration, why make an exception for Judaism? When the Falashas emigrated to Israel, they brought a certain amount of physical diversity, namely skin color, within the Jewish nation.

The Falashas are not the only dark-skinned Jews. The Lemba, a Bantu-speaking people of southern Africa, believe that they were led out of Judea by a man named Buba. They practice circumcision, keep one day a week holy, and avoid eating pork or pig-like animals such as the hippopotamus.[34] There is no Buba in the records in Jewish chronicles, but the proof of Jewish ancestry has been found by a team of geneticists, who discovered that many Lemba men carry on their Y-chromosome a DNA sequence, known as Cohen signature, that is distinctive of Jewish priests believed to be the descendants of Aaron, the older brother of Moses. The Y-chromosome is remarkable for two reasons. It is passed from father to son more or less unchanged, apart from an occasional mutation, and unlike the other chromosomes, its genetic material is not shuffled every generation, which obscures the lines of individual descent.[35]

There can be a very simple genetic explanation why this Y-chromosome is found in Bantu people who physically resemble their neighbors and why some Lemba men have it and others do not. It could be the result of what geneticists call the *founder effect*. Centuries ago a Jew, probably light-skinned, with this Y-chromosome mated with one or more of the dark-skinned Bantu women and converted them to Judaism. The males of this line inherited the Y-chromosome from him. Females of this line cannot pass it on, because women do not have a Y-chromosome, and their male offspring have a different Y-chromosome from their fathers, who were not related to the Jewish founder.[36]

IV. CHINA

A French Jew traveling in China desired to pray. Finding a synagogue, he entered. As he started to pray, he realized that the Chinese Jews were looking at him with apprehension and suspicion. After a few moments, the Chinese rabbi approached and asked what he wanted. The Frenchman said he had come to pray.
"But," the rabbi asked incredulously "are you Jewish?
"Of course, I am" replied the Frenchman. "That's odd," said the astonished rabbi, putting his hand to his slanted eyes, "You do not look it."

—Albert Memmi
Portrait d'un juif
[Translation by the author]

THE FIRST HISTORICAL REFERENCES TO JEWS IN CHINA WERE MADE by Arab geographers in the ninth and tenth century,[37] and in 1826 Marco Polo cites these communities as a powerful element in the political and economic life of China.[38] We do not know whether the original Jews brought wives with them, but probably not. They came as traders and likely took a Chinese concubine or wife. Their descendants had Chinese spouses and eventually became physically indistinguishable from the rest of the population. According to the Memorial of the Dead,[39] marriages between Jews and Chinese non-Jews took place on quite a large scale in the Ming dynasty. In China heritage is passed through the paternal line, so we may assume that the non-Jewish women adopted the husband's religion and raised their children as Jews. In the case of a Chinese husband and Jewish wife, their children would not be considered Jewish.

The Jewish communities were small and gradually disappeared, although the one in Kaifeng survived until the nineteenth century.[40] Over the centuries the Chinese Jews adopted the religions and cultures of their neighbors, mainly Islam, Confucianism, Buddhism, and Taoism, and a few became Christians.[41] The assimilation was complete, but their descendants with Jewish names are still labeled as such by the Chinese government which makes ethnic distinctions among its citizens.[42] Three reasons are given for this assimilation: total isolation from other Jews; a Chinese society, which accepted those who wanted to assimilate; and the Confucian tradition, especially marriage practices.

It would have been difficult for the Chinese Jews to resist assimilation. They perhaps numbered no more than 1,500 during most of their history, and contact with the outside world was limited for all Chinese by repeated wars, frequent flooding of the Yellow River, and the closed-door policy during the late Ming dynasty that restricted trade with the West. The isolation hindered Judaism in China because it prevented communicating with Jews in other lands and especially finding replacements for deceased rabbis.

Although China was tolerant of various ethnic and religious groups, from time to time the government required men of foreign extraction to marry women of Chinese extraction, and this may have caused some Jews to abandon their faith and traditions. Jews were permitted in the highest ranks of government, the academic world, and the military, but advancement generally hinged on civil service examinations, which required extensive knowledge of Confucian thought and literature. Adequate preparation meant years of study at Confucian schools, and in the case of Jews, that would come at the expense of Judaic schooling. Furthermore, a successful candidate usually was assigned to a post in a region far from home and a Jew would be even more isolated from his Jewish heritage.

Confucianism teaches that family rather than religion is the primary institution. One feature of Confucian marriage customs quite different from the Jewish tradition is that daughters should wed as early as possible. Social pressure of such customs may have prompted Chinese Jews to find non-Jewish spouses for their children, which would foster assimilation.[43] These marriage practices intensified in the nineteenth century, during which time the Jewish religion in China finally ceased to exist. Synagogues disappeared and circumcision was no longer practiced.

Such a thorough assimilation is said to be unique in Jewish history.[44] Individual Jews are often completely integrated into local society, but not an entire Jewish community. The unique Chinese Jewish culture is lost forever along any unique physical characteristics of the founders. Due to constant intermarriage, their descendants came to resemble all other Chinese. This is similar to what occurs in agricultural backcross breeding programs, when a plant with a certain characteristic is introduced into an established variety. For example, let us say the wheat variety *Wonder* is found susceptible to a newly introduced insect pest, but the variety *Bugproof* is resistant. Plant breeders crossed the two, and the offspring are then selected for their resistance to the insect. Those which pass the test are backcrossed to Wonder wheat, the process is repeated for six or seven generations, and eventually Wonder has its original qualities, plus resistance to the pest. There was no such intent in the case of the Jews of course, but after a few generations of intermarriage they became physically indistinguishable.

V. INDIA

In a narrow street of Cochin in the State of Kerala on the West Coast of India on a typical, hot humid day, you can spot people fairer than the rest. Their skin is light, and when they wear Western clothes, one is reminded of streets in London, Paris, or New York. Who are they? Suddenly they begin to speak in Malayalan, the language of the majority in Kerala. And the visitor is startled. The local people, however, find nothing incongruous. They have been accustomed to the presence of citizens of Jewish origin for over two thousand years, perhaps longer.

—T. V. Arasuram[45]
India's Jewish Heritage

READING THE ABOVE, ONE SHOULD NOT GET THE IMPRESSION THAT all the Jews of India had light skin; many of them had dark skin as other Indians. I am using the past tense because after the birth of the Jewish state, much of the Jewish population emigrated to Israel.

The contrast between fair and dark was a constant theme in the history of the Jews in India. The "black Jews" were treated by the "white Jews" with utmost contempt. The segregation between the two was very similar to that between blacks and whites in the U.S. and South Africa.[46] Marriage and social interaction between the two groups was forbidden. White Jews did not eat meat slaughtered by a black Jewish butcher. Children of a light-skinned father and a dark-skinned slave girl inherited the inferior status of the mother, in conformity with Hindu caste regulations.[47] The offspring of white slave owners and black female slaves in the United States had similar status.

There were three major Jewish communities in India: the Cochin Jews of the Malabar coast, the Bene Israel of western India, and the Baghadi (also called Iraqui) Jews of Bombay and Calcutta. Altogether they never numbered more than 30,000.[48] It is uncertain when the first Jews arrived. Most scholars believe they settled in the region of Kerala after the destruction of the Second Temple. Migration could have occurred much earlier, possibly after the Syrian conquest of Israel in 719 BCE or the conquest of Judea in 586 BCE, when some Jewish travelers found their way into Cranganore in southwest area and settled there.

Another story is that the first Jews reached India around 175 BCE, fleeing the persecutions of the Syrian ruler Antiochus Epiphanes. The boat that brought them was wrecked about 30 miles south of Bombay and only seven couples survived.[49] Their descendants, Bene Israel [Son of Israel], once formed the most important Indian Jewish group, but due to comparatively isolation, their Judaism lost much of its distinctiveness. They soon forgot Hebrew but continued to honor the Sabbath and other Jewish holidays, practiced circumcision, and kept the Jewish diet.[50]

The Bene Israel also adopted many Hindu customs, including the Indian caste system. Until recently, they tried to restrict marriage to their own community but they were not successful. Some Jews insist there has been no miscegenation with other peoples and the Bene Israel are "pure" Jews, but that is contradicted by their physical evidence: the completely "Indian" appearance and behavior. There has been considerable intermarriage with the

Hindu majority,[51] and there can be little doubt that the so-called black Bene Israel are the result of mixing with the native people.[52] In most cases, the father was Jewish and the Hindu mother had converted to Judaism. The Bene Israel are distinguished as black by Indian white Jews because to the latter the issue is important, the blacks are "impure" because they descend from non-Jewish mothers or from converts.

The Jews of the Malabar coast also have resided in India since ancient times, particularly in Cochin, 500 miles south of Bombay. According to tradition, their ancestors were left behind in King Solomon's time to gather cargo.[53] Being single men, they married native women and their descendants became the black Jews of Kerala. The white Jews of this city came mostly from Holland in the late fifteenth century, and each group had its own synagogues until 1900. The Cochin Jews maintained three endogamous, caste-like groups: black, white, and brown. Officially these did not intermingle,[54] but color variation within each group suggests otherwise.

The third Indian community, the Baghadi Jews, settled in Bombay around 1730.[55] They were considered white Jews, even though their skin color ranged from light to dark brown. This group included a small number of Europeans who immigrated before World War II, and hundreds more sought sanctuary during the Holocaust. Most of them left after the war and settled in Israel. Black Jews are also found among the Baghadi, the offspring of non-Jewish women, and the Baghadi claim there are only a few because intermarriage was frowned upon by both groups.[56] It should be noted that the Baghadi are physically less like the indigenous population than are the Bene Israel and Cochin Jews.

The considerable range of physical diversity among Indian Jews stems partly from their heterogeneous geographical origins, Spain and Portugal, Germany and Poland, Persia and Turkey, North Africa and Egypt, Babylonia and Syria, and Yemen and Mecca.[57] This diversity was increased by intermarriage with locals, conversion of slaves to Judaism, and polygamy. Both slavery and polygamy were common as late as 1843.[58] Wealthy Jews in Calcutta kept slaves of both sexes, sons born to women were circumcised.[59] Jewish masters usually manumitted slaves after a number of years. Once freed, they often chose to remain Jewish and tended to marry among themselves, but occasionally married other Jews.

Today, there are very few Jews left in India. They migrated to Israel for economic opportunities rather than for religious reasons.[60] They brought with them an array of physical characteristics, which once again belies the notion of a typically Jewish physiognomy.

VI. THE KHAZARS

In Khazaria, sheep, honey, and Jews exist in large quantities.
—Muquadassi
Descriptio Imperii Moslemici
Tenth Century[61]
Arthur Koestler, *The Thirteen Tribes*

One of the most interesting and most important cases of proselytism is that of the Khazars, who converted to Judaism in the eighth century. Very little is known about their origin and ultimate fate, but we know part of their history. Up to the end of the sixth century they wandered between the Volga and the Caucasus, but by the seventh century they controlled a wide region that is now in great part the Ukraine. Khazaria lay in the path of the Arab advance and this well-organized military power turned the tide of Arab invasion away from western Europe.[61] The Khazars were pagans, but for political reasons, could not remain so. In order to be united, they needed an ideological religious base.

In 740 CE, the Khazar rulers invited representatives of the three monotheistic religions—Catholicism, Islam, and Judaism—to make a case for their faith. After listening to them, the story goes, King Bulan decided to adopt Judaism. The historicity of this account is not proven, but it appears in both Arab and Jewish sources. It is likely that conversion to Judaism was progressive, from the kings to the nobility, to the rest of the population.[62] Although the Tamudic tradition remained largely unknown among the Khazars, they considered themselves "true" Jews and seem to have kept their faith for generations.

Some historians believe the Khazar kingdom fell in 969, defeated by the duke of Kiev, others claim it survived until the Tatar invasion of 1240.[63] Whatever the case, its inhabitants did not disappear. Most scholars assume that they found refuge in Jewish communities in eastern Europe or the Middle East. These historians do not agree[64] with Arthur Koestler who maintains that the Khazars were the ancestors of the majority of the East European Jews which makes them "more related to the Hun, Ulgur, and Magyar tribes than to the seed of Abraham, Isaac, and Jacob."[65]

Actually, we know very little about the ethnic origin of the Khazars, although they spoke a Turkic language, and from this we can infer that they were part of the Altaic world. We know virtually nothing about their physical appearance. Were they black-haired and swarthy? Were there "black" and "white" Khazars as the geographer Istaki suggests?[66] Did they have characteristics that we generally associate with Asian people, such as the Mongols? Regardless of how they looked, the Khazars were numerous and must have brought a considerable amount of biological diversity to the Jewish communities in which they took refuge.

10

Darkness at Noon

While the Jews of Spain basked in an Andulasian sunshine,
Christian Europe seethed with hatred. After the eleventh century the story of the Jewish life in France, England, and the
several hundred states of the Holy Roman Empire was a long
succession of indignities, brutalities, culminating in wholesale
massacres and expulsions.

—Abraham Leon Sachar
A History of the Jews

WHEN CHRISTIANITY BECAME THE OFFICIAL FAITH OF THE ROMAN
Empire, Judaism began to decline. Christianity was not suffi-
ciently sure of itself to show much tolerance toward any faith,
particularly Judaism, with which it shared many similarities. Judaism was regarded as a dangerous rival to be repressed, if not
suppressed. Beginning in 325 CE this attitude was expressed in a
succession of church councils whose edicts abrogated many
human rights of the Jews. For example, Jews could not own
slaves for fear they would attempt to convert them; they could
not marry Christians because they would have too much influence on their spouses and children; they could not be employed
as physicians by non-Jews because they would have too much
influence on their patients; they could not be appointed even to
unimportant posts because Christians should not be under the
civil control of Jews.

The measures were not uniformly enforced by local governments, which gained more and more power after of the Western
Roman Empire fell in the fifth century. Some jurisdictions were
very harsh, and others were very lenient for political or economic reasons.

In the east, the Greek-speaking Byzantine maintained power,
but Rome crumbled under the fierce assaults of Germanic and

Asiatic tribes ushering in the period historians once called the Dark Ages.[1] The Germanic kingdoms fell gradually to Christianity, and the Middle Ages began.

In the Middle Ages most of the people were peasants and were virtually slaves on land owned by the nobility or the church. Each family cultivated a plot whose tenancy passed from father to son. The feudal lord did not have the right to take away the land, but was owed rent money, food, and fodder. In addition, three days per week, the peasants had to work the lord's domain without compensation, whether tending fields and vineyards, repairing buildings and roads, or cleaning ditches and draining swamps. In the matter of justice they were at the mercy of the lord, who set fines and ordered punishment, including executions and confiscations. In time of war, which occurred frequently, peasants suffered not only from loss of life, but also from destruction of their fields and villages. There was no way to escape the oppressive hardship.

If the conditions were bad for most, they were worse for the Jews. Whether they lived in Eastern or Western Europe, the Jews became a hated, derided, and persecuted minority. Often they were flogged, dragged to the baptismal font, lost property through confiscation or ruinous taxes, and sometimes expelled or even executed. These conditions varied locally and changed over time. For example, in Provence and the Rhine Valley, Jews had the same rights as their neighbors, at least during the first thousand years of the Christian era.[2] They were freeborn, with the right to bear arms and acquire land, and they could participate in community affairs. On the other hand, in parts of France, Italy, and Spain,[3] anti-Judaism was very violent and often resulted in mass baptism or, if the Jews refused to be converted, in expulsion or death.[4]

The intensity of feeling in a particular area often changed with time, and there were periods of tolerance when marriage between Jews and non-Jews flourished. This was particularly true in Spain, which may be the cradle of modern racism but which also was the site of the greatest number of such intermarriages since the Roman Empire. After the Muslim conquest of Iberia, marriage was permitted between Moslem men and Christian or Jewish women.[5] The latter were thought to be more educated than Muslim women, and if education was important to Arab men, they married Jews but did not force them to adopt the Islam faith. Children of these unions were brought up in their father's faith, however, and many Ottoman sultans had Jewish mothers. Furthermore, in disobedience of Judaic law, Jewish men married non-Jews. Children of these unions as well as those born to their concubines were raised as Jews. The number of these offspring should not be underestimated, because concubinage was widespread before the fifteenth century.[6]

The authorities attempted to prevent sexual relations between Christians and Jews in the western world and imposed severe penalties on both partners, but they were not successful.[7] Support for this fact comes from frequent repetition of these laws, which indicates their ineffectiveness.[8] Many court cases in Italy involved violation of these laws as in Venice and Florence, where quite a number of Jews were tried and condemned for having sexual intercourse with Christian women, including nuns. Of course, many more cases were either undetected or not prosecuted. They left no trace in the documents, but often produced children of "mixed" parentage including the offspring of Jewish women raped by non-Jews. Such incidents were frequent, especially in localities where Jews were few and could offer no resistance. In 1418 an Italian Jewish conference condemned relations between Jewish men and Christian women, because it was feared that any children would be raised outside the Jewish faith.[9] Their fear was sound because the Jewish parent often lost custody.

Proselytism and conversion have always been part of both Christianity and Judaism. Jewish conversion during the Middle Ages may have occurred more frequently than has been reported. Jews continued to accept proselytes, and very important people were willing to convert to Judaism. Among them was Paul, a general in the Visigoth armies of King Wamba; Bodan-Elazar, a former deacon in the household of Louis the Pious, who fled to Spain in 839 and married a Jewish woman; and Vecelin, who in 1015 was the chaplain of Duke Conrad.[10] These men became energetic missionaries for their new faith. Others include the famous archbishop of Bari, who fled with part of his flock to Egypt, and the duke of Sens.[11]

People of less importance, willingly or unwillingly, also converted to Judaism, but we have no record because they were slaves owned by Jews. Their number is unknown, but may have been significant since the Council of Clichy passed an edict in 626 that punished Christians for selling slaves to Jews and Jews for owning slaves. Jews also attempted to convert their servants and workers.[12] Other proselytes were the ignorant Christian peasants who were told that their tax assessment would be reduced if they became Jews.[13] Armand Lunel suggests that at the beginning of the Middle Ages many illiterate pagans who desired to convert to Christianity confused the church with the synagogue and entered the door of the rabbi instead of the priest and became Jews.[14]

Christian proselytism also was very active. Records show that the church's early campaign to convert Jews met with some success, but progress was slow until the seventh century. In 629, the Merovingian King Dagobert issued a decree calling for the baptism or expulsion of all Jews from his domain. This ultimatum probably did more to gain converts to Christianity than any of the earliest efforts and it is believed that all the new converts remained Christians.[15] Conversion continued to be a high priority for the church, and a variety of documents suggest that clergymen were often successful in their efforts.[16] Sometimes these new Christians returned to their former faith, especially if they had converted under the threat of death or exile. Others were truly convinced of the superiority of Christianity and raised their children in the new faith.[17]

The more violent form of forced baptism occurred with the coming of the Crusades, which exemplified a new militance of Christendom against its foes. The goal of Pope Urban II and the great barons was a military expedition against Islam, but the First Crusades unleashed religious passions among the general public. It not only resulted in the conquest of Jerusalem, but also left a path of death and destruction within Christendom itself. Along the way to Palestine revenge upon the various infidels living in Christian territories and Jews were among the first victims if they did not agree to baptism. Some recanted immediately after the crusaders departed, and others remained Christian. Forced baptisms also occurred in Byzantium. These were part of an attempt by the Eastern Roman Empire to suppress all religious dissidence. Some Jews did become Christians, but most fled to Arabia.[18]

Despite its best efforts, the Catholic Church was unable to prevent the mingling of Jews and Christians that often led to intermarriage. As Leon Poliakov[19] jokingly remarked, "Mr. Israel Levy is as likely as his concierge to be a direct descendant of Vercingetorix."[20] This amalgamation would have introduced human diversity into both Christian and Jewish populations if they were biologically different. But that assumption is not valid in light of the history of the Jews just covered or events after the Middle Ages.

11

Ghetto Life in the Renaissance and Later

Dear God: Why did you send me such bad news this day of all days. I know, I know, we are the chosen people, but once in a while, could you choose someone else?
—Tevye, about the coming of a pogrom in his village. *Fiddler on the Roof*

LIFE FOR THE JEWS IN EUROPE GRADUALLY BECAME WORSE AFTER expulsion from England (1290), France (1394), and Spain (1492). Those who remained in these countries survived by posing as Christians, such as small groups of conversos in London and Bristol who secretly observed Jewish rituals. Some English Jews fled to the continent, and some who remained ceased to practice Judaism and ultimately were absorbed into the general population.[1] This was also the case for Portuguese and Spanish Jews who emigrated to the Bordeaux region of France at the beginning of the sixteenth century.[2] They professed Christianity, and many acquired wealth and social standing. They often married "Old Christians" and their children assimilated completely into the French culture. Two of them became famous: the philosopher Michel Montaigne and the poet François de Saigon. A number of descendants reverted in 1723 when Judaism was legalized.[3]

The statement that Jews were expelled from France in 1394 may be better understood if one recognizes that parts of modern France did not belong to the kingdom from which the Jews were expelled. One of these areas, the Contat Venaissin, was located between the Rhône and Durance rivers in Provence and belonged to the Holy See. It included the picturesque towns of Avignon and Carpentras, where a small number of Jews had settled before the Christian era. In 1394 they were joined by refugees expelled from the surrounding French provinces. At first the Jews were well treated by the papal authorities and they could own farms and houses wherever they pleased. As anti-Judaism grew, they reluctantly agreed to live within the confines of town ghettos, which they called carrières. The ghetto walls, originally intended to keep the victims in, were just as useful in keeping the enemies out. The concept of a separate quarter for Jews dated back a few centuries, and most major Islamic cities had one.

The story in Italy was similar. During the late fifteenth century there was an increase in the Jewish population due to the expulsion from Spain, and at first, they were welcomed. Then Naples fell to French and Spanish invaders. The papal states lost their tradition of tolerance, and the Inquisition was introduced. As in southern France, ghettos emerged in the sixteenth century, first in Venice, and then in major cities except Livorno (Leghorn). Venetian Jews were permitted to carry out their business by day, often at an inconvenient distance from home, but they were locked in at night. Further humiliations included wearing a distinctive badge and being compelled to listen to conversion sermons in their own synagogues. These miserable conditions remained in force until Napoleon conquered Italy in the nineteenth century.[4]

Life was even harsher for the Jews in Germany, where ghettos consisted of one or two narrow streets in the worst part of town, accessed through a single gate, that could be locked from the inside but not from outside. Due to the restricted sizes of ghettos, as the population grew, houses tended to be built higher and often met at the roofline. Overcrowding, squalor, and unsanitary conditions were endemic. Sunlight was sparse. Because the Jews could not own real estate, they were continually subject to gouging by Christian landlords. Ghetto life changed the character of Jewish society. Retreating within themselves, these communities strengthened their customs and their traditions. Proselytism and intermarriage ceased. The shift to a closed society was to be extremely important in Eastern Europe, where the majority of Jews soon lived.

As the doors of western Europe closed to the Jews, new doors were providentially opened elsewhere. Thousands of Jews found refuge in Turkey after being expelled from Spain and Portugal. They joined communities already established and brought with them their energy, knowledge, and talents. Poland became a refuge for Jews harried from Germany. An exodus from Germany started when the Crusaders destroyed the stability of German Jewish life. Polish rulers became less hospitable during the fifteenth century; they became less benevolent, pressured by non-Jewish merchants who resented the competition and by the Catholic Church which feared that Jews endangered the future of Christianity. Freedom became more restricted and eventually Polish Jews were forced to accept Christianity or to live in ghettos,[5] where they remained until 1868.[6]

Conditions were even worse for Jews in Russia, which was the least tolerant of the European powers. During the 1470s, in the rapidly expanding principality of Moscow, a semisecret sect, the Judaizers, was repressed with blood and fire. Czar Ivan Vasillievich, better known as Ivan the Terrible (1530–84), ordered the drowning of Jews who refused to embrace Christianity. Some rulers in the seventeenth century, such as Peter the Great, were more lenient, but the empresses who succeeded them were fanatic in their hatred of the Jews. Catherine in 1727, Anne in 1739, and Elizabeth in 1742 issued edicts that expelled the Jews from Russia. Ironically, successive partitions of Poland (1772, 1793, and 1795) gave Russia a large portion of that unfortunate country and with them a very large number of Jews perhaps equaling if not outnumbering all other Jewish populations combined.

Russian Jews were now confined to the newly acquired western provinces, the so-called Pale of Settlement, in order to prevent their spread to other parts of the empire. In 1835 the size was diminished, and Jews were excluded from all villages more than forty miles from the western frontier. In 1852, they were also expelled from the frontier area. This severe confinement destroyed their livelihood, and in this period a large number of Jews left Russia for western Europe and the United States.[7] Those who remained had to wait until the Bolshevik Revolution in March 1917 to enjoy the same human rights as their neighbors.[8]

Despite miserable living conditions, eastern Europe absorbed masses of Jewish immigrants from other countries and became the largest Jewish center in the world. At one time, roughly three quarters of the Jews in the world lived in Poland, Russia, Lithuania, Ukraine, Hungary, and Romania. They maintained their own religious institutions, were guided by their own clergy, spoke a common language (Yiddish), lived by a distinctive calendar, and rarely interacted with non-Jews. This may be the only time in the history of the Jews when marriage with others was a practical impossibility and when the conditions for race formation were present. However, these conditions lasted at the most 400 years, which represents only about 16 generations (assuming a generation span of 25 years). This is too short a time to produce any significant difference between Jews and non-Jews, no more than perhaps some loss in average height and physical vigor. Any change would amount to less than that observed in some villages in the European Alps, where marriages between cousins have been common for centuries. Furthermore, any minor change could be due to poor living conditions in the ghettos which stunted growth and favored the spread of infectious diseases. A large number of people died, and others survived having a good immune system. Inbreeding did foster the emergence of genetic diseases that persist in the Jewish population today.[9]

12

Liberty, Equality, and Fraternity?

Men are born and remained free and equal in rights . . . No
one can be harassed for his opinion, even religious, provided
that their manifestation does not disturb the law.
          —French Declaration of the Rights of Man, articles 1 and 6

With the french revolution, a new epoch dawned in europe.
The privileges of the church and nobility were abolished and the
freedom of conscience was proclaimed. The new attitude toward
oppressed minorities was remarkable. Among these were the
Jews, who had been victims of intense discrimination and
slaughtering for centuries.

In 1789 there were roughly 40,000 Jews in France, the majority
in the provinces of Alsace and Lorraine,[1] 3,500 in the Southwest,
and approximately 2,500 in the Contat Venaissin, and only 500
Jews could be found in Paris. Judaism was not practiced uniformly, and the Jews from Alsace and Lorraine were more Orthodox than those elsewhere. The Bordeaux community was
officially recognized as Jewish after more than a century of public adherence to Catholicism.[2] The civil status of Jews also differed. In Alsace, they were not permitted in town after sunset; in
Bordeaux, as professed Christians, they had the same rights as
other Frenchmen. When the Revolution came the Jews of the
Southwest became electors and one of them was almost elected
as a deputy to the Assembly.

Whereas the Jews around Bordeaux were politically minded,
the Jews of Alsace and Lorraine were only interested in improv-
ing their well-being. Their only request to the new government
was to be taxed the same as their non-Jewish neighbors, to be
free to do business, to be permitted to live wherever they wanted,
and to practice their religion without interference. Although not

119

all Jews in France asked to have equal political rights and French citizenship, they were granted both. It can be said that they received their emancipation without actually seeking it and without guarantee that they would be assimilated. In other words, the spirit of the Revolution played a far more important role than any effort by the Jewish communities.

When the revolutionary government declared the Jews and other minorities French citizens,[3] it was inspired by the underlying philosophy of the Rights of Man which can be summarized as:

> The national sovereignty belongs to all the people, not the king, nobles, or the clergy. The king and the social categories of the Old Order are therefore out. Free persons with equal rights compose France. These rights belong to the individuals, not their orders and not the state. Indeed the state represents the individuals and acts to protect their rights.[4]

These ideas were clearly in the mind of Clermont-Tonnerre, when he made this statement in support of the Jewish emancipation:

> Everything must be refused to the Jews as a nation; everything must be granted to them as individuals. Each of them should be individually a citizen. But it is claimed that they do not want this. Very well, let them say so, and they will have to be expelled. . . . There cannot be a nation within a nation.[5]

The Jews were granted equality in civil rights because they constituted not a national but a religious group within the ruling nation. They were not required to give up their ethnicity in order to be free and equal, but as the third part of the revolutionary slogan, many of their countrymen did not consider them as brothers. Anti-Semitism in France never died. Over the years it raised its ugly head more than once, such as during the Dreyfus affair and the Vichy regime.

Revolutionary France saw its mission as bringing human rights to all enslaved European people. Wherever the armies of the young republic penetrated, they brought the new gospel of the equality, and its corollary, Jewish emancipation. After the defeat of Napoleon, however, reactionary governments abrogated the edicts that had given Jews their freedom. Although free citizenship was granted in Prussia in 1812, in other parts of Germany, Jews had to wait until the German Reich (1871) to obtain equal status before the law. Prior to that, they faced widespread social and occupational discrimination, particularly in the diplomatic corps, the army, the civil service, and the universities.[6] In the Austrian Empire (including Hungary) only after the Revolution of 1848 did marriage and resident restrictions disappear.[7]

Sooner or later, the Jews of Western Europe were allowed to leave the ghettos in which they had been imprisoned throughout the Middle Ages. They were free to attend the same schools, wear the same clothes and engage in the same activities as their neighbors. It became impossible to tell who was a Jew. Intermarriages occurred which anti-Semites regarded as a terrible threat to the "pure Aryans." These unions were made easier by the French Revolution, which transformed marriage from a religious to a civil act and the practice of civil marriage spread throughout Europe.

Jewish conversion to Christianity also increased with emancipation. This may seem odd because traditionally conversion had been an escape from persecution, and emancipation should have made that unnecessary. Anti-Semitism remained, however, and many Jews regarded their religion as a misfortune and came to hate it. Psychologically, the choice became easier as society became more secular, and conversion could be viewed less as a religious act than a social opportunity. Heinrich Heine (1797–1856) contemptuously referred to this as an "entrance-ticket to European society."[8] It has been said that a man felt he had to become a Christian in the nineteenth century in the same way he felt he had to learn English in the twentieth century. In fact, during the nineteenth century, at least 250,000 Jews bought their entrance tickets.[9]

Intermarriage between persons became easier because of civil marriage, but consequently more difficult to quantify, because many jurisdiction did not require information about the religion of the participants. Even when such data is available, it may not be useful, because one of the spouses may have converted prior to the wedding. Nevertheless, the high degree of assimilation of Jews in France and Germany after 1789 suggests these unions were substantial in number. It is estimated that 6 percent of

Jews married in Paris between 1808 and 1860 wed Christians.[10] By the 1870s the figure was 12 percent.[11] In Germany at the turn of the century 8 percent of the Jews married non-Jews.[12] The proportion reached 12 percent a decade later and in 1930 nearly one-fifth of Jews married persons of another faith. In large cities the rate was even greater. In Berlin in 1929, the figure was 25 percent[13] and possibly even 65 percent.[14] In Hamburg, intermarriage rose to 33.4 percent in 1928. Most of the children of these unions were not raised as Jews.[15]

Trends were similar in other parts of Europe. In 1933, the rate of intermarriage in Bohemia was 28 percent,[16] and in Italy it was even higher 56.1 percent.[17] In Sweden, despite anti-Semitic laws, there was so much intermarriage that an 1873 ordinance stipulated that children born to Jewish-Christian couples must be brought up Lutheran.[18] In Denmark,

> the Jewish population has not increased in the sixty years from 1840 to1901, but has decreased absolutely and even more relatively, most likely. In 1840 0.3% of the total population was still Jewish; in 1901 only 0.14. The proportion of Jews has decreased therefore by more than one half. The reason is not only the small number of children, but chiefly the numerous mixed marriages by means of which the Danish Jews are being gradually absorbed by the non-Jewish population.[19]

In England intermarriage was intense for three centuries, most likely because Jews integrated into mainstream society with less resistance compared to other European states.[20] Many Jews moved in Christian circles with an ease common elsewhere only centuries later,[21] and the British had a prime minister of Jewish descent. Spanish Jews who immigrated to England in the seventeenth century, however, remained second-class citizens until 1858, being excluded from universities, the bar, local governments, and Parliament.[22] After 1858 Jews were socially integrated within a few years.[23]

Political and social conditions were in general so favorable in England from the age of the Enlightenment to the period of World War II that perhaps several hundred thousand Jews abandoned their faith.[24] Some embraced Christianity outright and others drifted away due to intermarriage or religious indifference.

English Jews who converted tended to be insensitive to the spiritual claims of either religion. Once baptized, former Jews were able to marry into the gentry and noble families, serve in local government, enter Parliament, and mix freely in elite cultural and social circles. It is impossible to know for certain the size of this group. The Church of England was disinterested in gathering statistics from local parishes on the number of Jews who converted or married Christians without formally converting.[25]

There was never complete emancipation of the Jews in Eastern Europe, even in post-Revolution Russia. The Jews in the Soviet Union were given rights as a group, the same as any other minority. These rights were never well defined. Furthermore, because all religion was banned, they were not free to practice Judaism. Synagogues were closed down or converted into clubs and public religious teaching was prohibited. In addition, Judaism was not only considered a religion, but also a nationality. Like other citizens, Jews had to carry a passport that showed name, date of birth, nationality, permanent residence, and place of work. The word "Everei" appeared on their passports. If both parents had the same nationality the children automatically assumed it. If the parents were of different nationality, the child at age 16 selected one of the two.[26] Passports had to be produced in the Soviet Union when one applied for a job, admission to a school, and so on. National and ethnic prejudices often operated in bureaucratic decisions, and Jewish designation was often used to block access to employment, promotion, or schooling. As in France, the revolution did not eradicate anti-Semitism and under Stalin in the late 1940s and early 1950s a portion of the Jewish intelligentsia was murdered. It was very difficult to leave the Soviet Union, the only escape from anti-Semitism was to renounce Judaism and marry a non-Jew. Nearly half the marriages among Jews involved a non-Jewish partner.[27]

Since World War II the tendency for Jews to marry non-Jews is increasing. This is especially true in the United States—the subject of the next chapter—where some fear that intermarriage will lead to the eventual disappearance of Jewish communities.

13

Jews in the United States

The high rate of intermarriage between Jews and non-Jews
has to do with where we live and what we do . . . and as long
as we don't live in ghettos, we are going to intermarry.

—Rabbi Stephen Foster

RABBI FOSTER IS CORRECT. IN AMERICA JEWS NEVER WERE CONFINED
in ghettos, and today many live in suburbs among non-Jews. This
freedom explains why the rate of intermarriage in the United
States was always high and continues to increase compared to
Europe.[1] As Samuel Hellman points out:

> Today is a time when American Jews experience a minimum of prej-
> udice, when all domains of life are open to them. But it is also a time
> of extraordinary assimilation, of swelling rates of intermarriage and
> of large numbers of people simply ignoring their Jewishness com-
> pletely.[2]

The first Jews to gather in North America came from Brazil
in 1654. Twenty-three in number, they sailed aboard the *Sainte
Catherine* and landed in the town of New Amsterdam (later, New
York). By 1800 the Jewish population in the United States had
reached only 2,500.[3] Although for the most part excluded from
voting and holding office before the Revolution, the Jews mingled
freely with non-Jews and very often intermarried. Incredible as
it may seem, it is reported that every Jew who settled and remained in Connecticut before the Revolution married a Christian.[4] According to Malcom Stern almost 16 percent of the Jews
in North America before 1840 married Christians.[5] Some maintained their affiliation with the Jewish community, and the
spouses of a few converted to Judaism, but the vast majority who
intermarried were assimilated.

124

The high rate of intermarriage reflects two situations in colonial America. First, the small number of Jews widely scattered had limited marriage options. Second, Jews were far less ostracized in the New World than in the Old because people, whatever their ethnic origin, were needed to propel economic growth and this necessity reduced social barriers. The American Revolution, like the French Revolution, brought to the Jews the rights of citizenship, and they gradually achieved full participation in civic affairs.[6]

As late as 1820 there were only about 4,000 Jews in the United States.[7] Then, the surge of Jewish immigration from Europe began, and marriage patterns changed somewhat. There were ample opportunities to choose Jewish mates in the Eastern parts of the United States, but far fewer in the West where Jewish men continued to intermarry sometimes with native Americans or Mexicans.[8]

Especially in eastern cities, the proximity to other ethnic groups led to some intermarriage. In the late nineteenth century, hundreds of Jewish girls wed sons of Italian immigrants each year.[9] In the 1920s, films were projecting the view that it was acceptable for the beautiful daughter of an Irish policeman to marry the loving and talented son of a Jewish merchant. Many Jewish film producers, directors, and writers had non-Jewish wives.[10] As Jewish men climbed the ladder of the corporate, financial, and academic world, they no longer lived in an exclusively Jewish environment, and the inevitable result was often intermarriage and an attenuation of Jewish identity. Nevertheless, until the mid twentieth century, the intermarriage rate was less than 10 percent.

Today, more Jews marry non-Jews (52 percent) than marry within their religion.[11] Such an increase is not astonishing in view of the decline in anti-Semitism in the United States, court cases that ended discrimination and ensured freedom of association, and changes in residential patterns, which mean that Jews and non-Jews attend public school together, date, and marry. According to Robert Gordis, "Intermarriage is part of the price that modern Jewry must pay for freedom and equality in an open society."[12] Furthermore, an open society allows not only freedom of choice in religion but also the freedom to have none. Among those who no longer identify themselves with any religious group, more than one million of those individuals were born into Jewish families.[13]

14

A Summary Why Jews Are Not a Race: History and Biology

> Hardly any aspect of life is more characteristic than its almost unlimited diversity. No two individuals in sexually reproducing populations are the same, no two populations of the same species, not two species of two higher taxa, nor any associations, and so on ad infinitum. Wherever we look, we find uniqueness, and uniqueness spells diversity.
>
> —Ernst Mayr

THE HISTORY OF THE JEWS, WHICH INCLUDES INTENSIVE PROSELY-tism and marriage with non-Jews, explains why it is impossible to distinguish a Jew physically from a non-Jew.

I say "physically" because some Jews are said to exhibit a certain appearance, but this "look" is common among peoples of the Near and Middle East. Ashley Montagu has developed this idea:

> One will often go wrong and mistakenly identify as Jews persons of non-Jewish origin, such as many Italians, Greeks, Turks, Arabs, Berbers, and related people. The quality of looking Jewish is not due so much to any inherited characters of the persons in question as to certain culturally acquired habits of expression, facial, vocal, muscular and mental. Such habits do, to an impressive extent, influence the appearance of the person and in large part determine the impression he makes upon others. Whether such persons will be identifiable as "Jews" will depend upon the character of the population among which they live.[1]

The history of the Jews also explains why scientists have failed to find any meaningful biological differences under the skin between Jews and non-Jews. In their search for distinctions, scientists turned to population genetics and polymorphism, which

126

refers to the occurrence of two or more genetic variants of the same trait within a given population. The vast majority of these variants are blood groups and electrophoretic variants of certain plasma proteins. Geneticists use these numerous polymorphic systems in man as genetic markers to trace the evolution, migration, and structures of populations.

In 1950 hope was high that differences among humans would be found using blood groups which genetically are relatively simple and well understood. They are determined at birth and are not affected by the environment. Unlike the visible characteristics, they have the further practical advantage that their consideration is unaffected by an emotional history.

Blood consists of a number of things, two of which are the most important for our discussion. These are the red blood cells which transport oxygen, and serum, a yellow fluid containing antibodies that defend the body against diseases. At the beginning of the twentieth century, it was discovered that some people have red blood cells that carry substance A. Others have red blood cells that carry substance B. The cells of some individuals carry both substances or neither. Substances A and B eventually were called antigens and more than sixty other types of antigens have been discovered. Blood groups can be sharply differentiated by a simple objective test. As a result, millions of such determinations are made every year, which provides a wealth of information about blood group distribution in humans around the world. Within each blood group, human populations often differ in their genetic make up, that is, in the frequency of certain forms of genes (alleles). For example, in relation to the ABO blood group, population X could have the following frequencies, A#0.4; B#0.1; 0#0.5, whereas another population, Y, could have the frequencies A#:0.3; B#0.2; 0#0.5. The ABO blood group is widely used in human population studies, but so are two others, the MN and the Rh blood groups. Although data are easy to obtain, the results are not easy to interpret.

For example, analysis of ABO and MN blood group data shows in general that Jews in a given location tend to resemble the non-Jews in that location, and the frequency of certain genes in some Jewish populations is different from other Jewish populations that are geographically distant.[2] Yet, Jews show greater uniformity in their Rh gene frequencies than in ABO and MN frequencies. Should we conclude, with Mourant, that Jews from Europe, who are scarcely distinguishable from their former European non-Jewish neighbors by their ABO group, show by their Rh group that they are more closely related to their Mediterranean ancestors?[3]

There are serious problems with the interpretation of population genetics data. First, we do not know how different the frequency of a particular gene in one population has to be from another population in order to be meaningful? Second, in many studies there is no control group. This is very important, because two samples of the same population may differ in gene frequency. For our purpose, we would need at least two samples from the Jewish population and two samples from the non-Jewish population.

Also it would be very helpful to know the genetic blood composition of the original Jews of Palestine, but this is not possible because at best only skeletons remain. One approach might be to extract DNA from ancient bone and compare it to DNA from non-Jews. But, to my knowledge, this technique has not been tried.

Another problem in searching for genetic differences among Jews and between Jews and others is the question: Who is a Jew? According to the Halacha (Jewish Law) one is a Jew through maternal heritage or conversion. The latter is a religious definition of who is a Jew is of little help in genetics. Jewish historians, linguists, anthropologists, and geneticists have not produced a unified definition that is acceptable to all.

Classification of Jewish communities is also very difficult because many dynamic events have molded these groups. Various migrations and exposure to such forces as religious conversion, assimilation, and intermarriage complicate the issue. Most Jewish communities today represent a mixture of a common ancestral population with the various groups among whom the Jews have lived since the diaspora.

To understand why it is so difficult to read the genetic data from human populations, let us turn to the basic principles of population genetics.

A population is a group of individuals living in the same locality and freely interbreeding with one another. The sum total of the genes carried by all the individuals is known as the gene pool.

Each newborn has a small sample of the genes in this pool. According to the famous Hardy–Weinberg principle, the frequency of the traits will remain the same if mating occurs at random and if there is neither mutation nor selection. Of course, such an ideal population does not exist, for mutation always occurs and is the source of variability. What concerns us most are the mating habits in a human population, for they can seriously influence the frequency of genes.

In random mating such factors as appearance or social customs do not influence the choice of mates. But preferential mating, for example, Jews marrying Jews, can result in subgroups of different types in a population.[4] Human populations can remain distinct, however, only when various groups are separated by some sort of barrier that prevents free interbreeding. In human history no barrier has been so great as to prevent some gene flow, or the introduction of new alleles into a population. This has been an important factor in bringing about alterations of human gene pools. When two populations live adjacent to one another, such as on the border of two countries, there has always been some gene flow between them. Sexual attraction is such that no political, social, or religious restrictions can prevent intermarriage or clandestine sexual contact. For many centuries the Jews lived within other populations and tried to maintain the purity of their gene pool by strong religious restrictions against marriage to those of a different faith. They were successful in some degree, but some gene flow occurred nevertheless. That is why the descendants of Spanish Jews living in New York City have a distinct difference in the proportion of certain forms of genes from the descendants of the German Jews in that city, and both groups differ from the descendants of the Romanian Jews.

Immigration and foreign invasion can bring about considerable gene flow. The great number of people (including Jews) who have come to the United States have introduced genes from all over the world. Foreign armies always leave progeny as a result of rape or voluntary sexual relationships and some soldiers who may have liked the country so well that they marry into the local population.[5]

Genetic drift, another factor responsible for a change in gene frequencies, happens sometimes when the number of mating pairs in a population is small. The gene frequency in a small population may change because of chance fluctuation. The change is related to the fact that the sex cells which produce a generation are not a representative sample of the population. There is no doubt that genetic drift played an important role when some Jewish populations were nearly exterminated. An extreme example of genetic drift is the founder principle. Sometimes a new population is founded by a very small sample from a larger one. A small group may set off to a distant new home, and the proportion of genes it carries is not likely to be the same as in the large population from which it comes. The founder effect has been cited as the reason for certain genetic diseases among the Ashkenazim.[6]

Despite all these difficulties, interpretations of genetic data about the Jews stresses two themes: 1) An intrinsic admixture of different non-Jewish populations with Jews, which resulted in great heterogeneity among Jewish groups, and 2) A common Middle Eastern origin.[7] In addition, in the early 1980s the study of human variation at the gene level emerged. Differences in the prevalence of diseases and other genetic markers between Jews and non-Jews and among various Jewish communities became particularly prominent during the massive migration to Israel from all over the world, which began in 1948 and continues. These studies indicated that the "genetic distance"[8] among major Jewish groups of diverse geographical origins were often smaller than the distance between Jews and non-Jews of the same regions, with the exception of those of Jews from Yemen, India, and Ethiopia. These three Jewish populations tended historically to be isolated. Such findings have provoked lively discussion and even controversies among historians and population geneticists about the processes involved in these differences and similarities.[9]

These differences, if they exist, are not great enough to consider Jews and non-Jews two distinct groups of human beings. Most alleles at most polymorphic sites are present in all populations. Their frequencies differ, allowing us to make some inferences on population relationships, but no allele at an individual site serves as a marker for a phylogenetically distinct subset (race) of the species.[10] Even if the frequency of a gene form in one population was 1.00 (100%) and 0.00 (0 %) in another, the two populations would differ by only one gene out of 30,000.[11]

Perhaps the most important point in this debate lies in the frequency of genetic diseases in some groups of Jews and non-Jews. However, a number of sociological changes are occurring in Europe and the United States: increased intermarriage among the Jewish communities decreased consanguinity, and increased marriage with non-Jews. These changes undoubtedly will reduce the rate of genetic diseases and the diversity between Jews and non-Jews, if such diversity exists at all.

Conclusion

Human history becomes more and more a race between education and catastrophe.

—H. G. Wells

IN SPRING 1995, MY WIFE AND I WERE INVITED BY ONE OF HER LONG-
time friends to attend the bar mitzvah of a grandson in Ann
Arbor, Michigan. About half the audience in the synagogue was
not Jewish. This was because the mother's family was Jewish,
but the father's family was not.

I looked around me trying to guess which was which. Some
men wore their yarmulke and probably are Jewish, but I cannot
be sure because once I saw President Clinton on television wearing a yarmulke when he visited a synagogue in New York. I cannot say anything about the women who wore modern clothes.

For the first time in my life I heard prayers in Hebrew. If the
prayers had not been translated into English in the program we
were given, I would have had no notion of what was being said.
They extolled peace and love for mankind. Looking around the
audience of Jews and non-Jews sharing a Saturday morning of
joy with a boy, I was more than ever driven to finish this book.

Despite my long conviction that Jews are not a separate race
of human beings, writing the book has not been easy. It was clear
to me that if Jews were never sexually isolated, conditions for the
formation of a distinct race could not occur, but to support my
thesis I had to turn to their history, of which I had practically no
knowledge at the time. Today, I am far from being an expert on
the subject, but I know enough to be sure that Jews from time
immemorial were never isolated, that they intermarried, and
that Jewish law always allowed converts. Only the European
ghettos provided the proper conditions for race formation, but
that period of isolation was not long enough to have any lasting
effect. Jews elsewhere remained free to intermarry, absorb con-

verts. Genetic interchange and conversion explain why it is impossible to distinguish Jews from non-Jews by appearance. The Nazis thought there was a physical difference, but they had to pass a law that required Jews to wear a yellow star on their outer clothing. Of course, this lack of ability to distinguish a Jew from non-Jew has never stopped anti-Semitism. Indeed, anti-Semites reproach them for hiding their Jewishness within the population at large.

Reading about Jews led me to a surprising conclusion. I cannot supply the statistics, but I am convinced that throughout the ages a far larger number of people abandoned the Jewish faith than adhered to it. For all kinds of reasons: personal, political, economical, and sheer survival. Jews converted, intermarried, and raised their children as non-Jews.[1] This was true from Babylonian captivity to modern times. This integration of so many Jews in the mainstream makes a mockery of the contamination that anti-Semites fear. If it were true, the harm would have been done long ago, and society would be beyond repair.

Another finding is that the lack of distinguishing "racial traits" forced the French and German Nazis, to define the Jews by socio-religious criteria, that is, how many grandparents were Jewish. Some Nazis seem to have been very well aware that the race theory could not be supported. The following is from a report prepared by Dr. Richard Korherr for his boss, Henrich Himmler, dated March 2, 1943:

> Until recently, statistics hardly ever distinguished Jews by race, but by religious faith. For the establishment of racial origins, many years of training are needed, as well as the investigation of ancestry. The establishment of race affiliation has been found to be particularly difficult in southern and eastern countries, for, in spite of all efforts, it has proved impossible to define a uniform single Jewish race. The adherence to the Mosaic or Israelite religion cannot serve any more as complete valid proof. Due to the Jewish missionary movement, which in the past has used the proselyting in the modern era, whether by mixed marriage or persuasion, there lived today as many Faith Jews who do not belong to the Jewish race as those who do. On the other hand, the number of Jews has been reduced by forced conversion as well as voluntary conversions, which became much more frequent in recent times, and also by the phenomenon of communally unaffiliated persons of the Jewish race.[2]

Today, anti-Semites seem more sophisticated. A contemporary Nazi, Jean-Marie Le Pen, head of the French National Front, claims there is a Jewish race. But one of his lieutenants, Pierre Vial, denies it. He said: "Of course there is no Jewish race in the anthropological sense, no more than there is a French or German race."[3]

Ironically, anti-discrimination rulings and wider acceptance of Jews have done far more to challenge the cohesiveness of Jewish communities than overt persecution. Mob violence, bureaucratic harassment, legal discrimination, and social exclusion took their toll in emotional distress and destruction of lives and property. But it is in liberal nations of the West, that Jewry as a body has started to erode. Emancipation brought unambiguous benefits to Jews as individuals but not to Jews collectively or to Judaism as a culture and religion. According to Alan Dershowitz,[4] the most serious threats today come not from persecutors, but from those who may kill the Jews with kindness by assimilating them.

Two historians have opposite views of the future of Judaism. Simon Rawidowicz rejects the self-imposed image of the Jewish people as being on the verge of disappearing,[5] whereas Norman Cantor argues that the Jewish history is approaching its end.[6] According to him, the Jews have fulfilled their role. Giving the world three great religions Judaism, Christianity, and Islam—Cantor is sure that the Jewish heritage will endure even if the Jews as a group disappeared in the twenty-first century.

Whatever the future, Jews today have never been less socially isolated, especially in the United States. The rates of assimilation and intermarriage are at their highest. What biological changes, if any, will these social conditions bring? If the Jews disappear through assimilation and intermarriage, three important biological effects can be expected. First, the frequency of certain forms of genes more prevalent in Jewish populations will increase in non-Jewish populations, which means more diversity in individuals. Secondly, the difference between Jews and non-Jews will be enhanced because the number of intramarriage partners for the remaining Jews will shrink. Third, certain genes will become more concentrated in this smaller group due to chance fluctuations. An individual who happens to carry a particular allele may have more children than his neighbors or he may have none.

CONCLUSION 135

Changes will vary across nations. For example, in the United States, Jews who remain Jews may become very slightly genetically different from the larger population in which they live. Whereas in Israel diversity will remain high, because Jews have immigrated there from all over the world. It is harder to predict what may happen in France, where a large number of Orthodox Jews emigrated after World War II and joined the descendants of French Jews who had escaped the Holocaust.

I have discovered that both Jewish and non-Jewish writers find it difficult to accept the idea that Judaism is simply a religion and that Jews who abandon the faith are no longer Jews.

Michael Curtis writes:

> We beseech all Christians to renounce every kind of antisemitism, and earnestly oppose it, if it stirs anew, and to encounter both Jews and *Jewish Christians*."[7] (italics mine)

May I ask what are Jewish Christians? According to Pierre Birnbaum:

> Although French Jews, whether religious or not, are more likely than non-Jews to vote for candidates of the center and center left.[8]

If they are not religious Jews, they are not Jews, and Birnbaum could have written:

> French Jews and individuals of Jewish ancestry. are more likely than the rest of the population to vote for candidates of the center and center left.

My reading also made me realize that many victims of anti-Semitism, like those of any type of racism, unconsciously believe the propaganda, namely, that they are biologically different, that they are members of a distinct race. Cantor is convinced that this is why Jews have innate superior intellectual qualities, which:

> will be perpetuated by intermarriage through the bloodlines of millions of people and diffused through American, Arab, and other societies. Their intermarriage with scions of the Wasp elite in the United States will generate a new American patrician class, part Jewish, as

occurred in Iberia in the sixteenth century among families partly descended from Jewish converts.[9]

The idea that Jewishness is inherited lingers in such expressions as "I was born a Jew" and "I am a half Jew."[10] when one should say instead: "I was born in a Jewish family" and "my father or my mother is/was Jewish."

More than fifty years after Hitler's death, some still refer to "non-Aryan people," although the Aryan race is a myth.[11] Jews are neither a race nor a nation. Israel is a nation: Jews in England, France, the United States, and so on, are citizens of their countries. Jews belong to a religious federation: it is their religion that separates them from the rest of the world.

By rejecting the notion of a Jewish race and claiming that a Jew is simply someone who follows the Judaic rites, I am faced with a dilemma. How do I explain that there are some people who, like my brother, Gilles, who are not religious, but claim to be a Jew. I am inclined to believe their claim is based on a fondness for cultural tradition and a feeling of solidarity with the victims of anti-Semitism. Whatever their reason, it is their choice, and not the criterion of some Hitler who classifies them according to absurd pseudo-biological rules. If my brother wants to be a Jew, that is his choice. If I do not want to be a Jew, it is mine.

Notes

PREFACE

1. Alain F. Corcos, *The Little Yellow Train: Survival and Escape from Nazi France. June 1940–1944* (Tuscon, AZ: Hats Off Books, 2004).
2. R. Saraute and P. Tager, *Les juifs sous l'occupation. Recueil des textes officiels français et allemands* (Paris: Centre de documentation juive contemporaine [CDJC], 1982.
3. See the American Anthropological Association statement on race in *Anthropology Newsletter* 39 (September 1998): 1.
4. Alain F. Corcos, *The Myth of Human Races* (East Lansing: Michigan State University Press, 1997).
5. Karl Kautsky, *Are the Jews a Race?* 1914. (English Translation updated by the author, 1926) (Westport, CT: Greenwood, 1972); and Raphael Patai and Jennifer Patai Wing, *The Myth of the Jewish Race* (New York: Charles Scribner's Sons, 1975).

INTRODUCTION

1. Ellen Jaffe McClain, *Embrace the Stranger* (New York: Basic Books. 1995), 138.
2. Mark Visniak, *An International Convention against Antisemitism* (New York: Research Institute of The Jewish Labor Committee, 1945).
3. Simon Weisenthal, *Sails of Hope. The Secret Mission of Christopher Columbus* (New York: Macmillan Publishing Co., 1973), 112.
4. Chaim Lipschitz, *Franco, Spain, the Jews, and the Holocaust* (New York: KTAV Publishing House, Inc., 1984), 40.
5. Paul Johnson, *A History of the Jews* (New York: Harper and Row, 1987). See also Cecil Roth, *History of the Jews from the Earliest Times through the Six Day War* (New York: Schoken Books, 1970), 7, 37.
6. Ellie Kedourie, *Spain and the Jews* (London: Thames and Hudson, 1990), 156.
7. Alex Bein, *The Jewish Question: Biography of a World Problem* (Madison, NJ: Fairleigh Dickinson University Press, 1990), 24.
8. Ibid., 20.
9. John Dippell, *Bound Upon a Wheel of Fire* (New York: Basic Books, 1996).
10. Sidney Shapiro, *Jews in Old China* (New York: Hypocrene Books, 1984).

11. Michel Abitol, *The Jews of North Africa during the Second World War* (Detroit, MI: Wayne State University Press, 1989).

12. John Gager, *The Origins of Anti-Semitism: Attitudes toward Judaism in Pagan and Christian Antiquity* (New York: Oxford University Press, 1985), 147.

13. William Saffran, "Perceiving and Reaching to Antisemitism," in *Antisemitism in the Contemporary World*, ed. Michael Curtis (Boulder, CO: Westview Press, 1986), 274.

14. Paul Colongue, "L'antisémitisme à l'époque Bismarkienne et l'attitude des Catholiques allemands," in *De l'antijudaisme à l'antisémitisme contemporain* (Lille: Presses de l'Université de Lille, 1975), 150.

15. Leon Poliakov, *The History of Antisemitism* (New York: Vanguard Press, 1965–1975), 446.

16. Michael Beschloss, *The Conquerors: Roosevelt, Truman and the Destruction of Hitler's Germany, 1941–1945* (New York: Simon & Schuster, 2002), 243.

17. David Gerber, *Antisemitism in American History* (Urbana: University of Illinois Press, 1986), 19.

18. Leonard Dimmerstein, *Anti-Semitism in America* (New York: Oxford University Press, 1994), xxii.

19. Todd Endelman, *Radical Assimilation in English Jewish History 1665–1945* (Bloomington: Indiana University Press, 1990), 44.

20. Nora Levin, *The Jews in the Soviet Union since 1917* (New York: New York University Press, 1988), 23.

21. Anonymous (Reuters), "Hidden from the Nazis. He speaks for German Jews" *New York Times*, January 10, 2000.

22. Safran, *Perceiving*, 110.

23. Cited in Samuel C. Heilman, *Portrait of American Jews. The Last Half of the 20th Century* (Seattle: University of Washington Press, 1955), 111–12.

24. Gerald Sorin, *A Time for Building: The Third Migration 1880–1920*, vol. 3, *The Jewish People in America*. ed. Henry Feingold (Baltimore: Johns Hopkins University Press, 1992), 11.

25. Paula Hyman, *The Jews in Modern France* (Berkeley: University of California Press, 1998), 56.

26. Katja Azoulay, *Black, Jewish, and Interracial: It is Not the Color of Your Skin, but the Race of Your Skin and Other Myths of Identity* (Durham, NC: Duke University Press, 1997).

INTRODUCTION TO PART I

1. The bacterium *Micrococcus prodigus*, which in contact with the air produces a blood-like stain on certain foods, including the wafer, was the cause of many medieval pogroms.

2. The word anti-Semite was coined by a Jewish scholar (Moritz Steinschneider) in a polemic against the French writer, Ernest Renan. The term was taken up in 1879 by Wilhelm Marr, a German pamphleteer, and used as a purely political concept aimed quite unequivocally not at the speakers of other Semitic languages, but specifically and exclusively at the Jews. The ideas which Marr labeled anti-Semitic were widespread in Germany and Austria in the

nineteenth century, particularly among the anti-liberal, anti-modern, nationalist political parties and movements that were gaining in influence at the time. See Joe Carmichael, *The Satanizing of the Jews* (New York: Fromm International Publishing Company, 1992).

3. Among them are Leon Poliakov, Hanna Arendt, and Jacques Maritain.

4. Benzion Netanyahu, *The Origins of the Inquisition in Fifteenth-Century Spain* (New York: Random House, 1995).

5. M. Simon, *Verus Israel* (Paris: De Brocard, 1964). See also A. N. Sherwin White, *Racial Prejudice in Imperial Rome* (Cambridge: Cambridge University Press, 1967), 99.

6. As defined by John Efron in *Defenders of the Race, Jewish Doctors and Race Science in Fin du Siècle Europe* (New Haven: Yale University Press, 1994), 5.

7. Because so many Jews did not resemble the stereotype and escaped detection, one would think that this knocks the props out from under anti-Semitism, but it only serves as an added grievance: the Jews are said to conceal themselves cunningly.

8. Marc Hillel, *Au nom de la race* (Paris: Fayard, 1975).

9. Bruce Jackson, *Law and Disorder* (Urbana: University of Illinois Press, 1984).

10. See Bernard Lewis, *Semites and Anti-Semites, An Inquiry into Conflict and Prejudice* (London: Norton & Co., 1986); Helen Fey, *The Persisting Question* (Berlin and New York: Walter de Gyter, 1987), 424; and Valentin Nikiprowetsky, ed., *De l'antijudaisme à l'antisémitisme contemporain* (Paris: Presses Universitaires, 1985), 15.

CHAPTER 1. THE JEWISH RACE

1. Carlos Levy. "L'antijudaisme paien. Essai de synthèse." In *De l' Antijudaisme à l'antisémitisme contemporain* (Lille: Presses Universitaires de Lille, 1975).

2. German historians during the Nazi period attempted to demonstrate that "racial" anti-Semitism dated from the antiquity, but they failed. Jules Isaac, *Genèse de l'antisémitisme* (Paris: Calmann-Levy, 1956).

3. Julian Rinehart Huxley, "Race in Europe," *Pamphlets in World Affairs* (New York: Farrar and Rinehart Inc., 1939).

4. Sherwin White, *Racial Prejudice in Imperial Rome* (Cambridge: Cambridge University Press, 1967), 6.

5. Levy, "L'antijudaism paien," 52.

6. Hugo Valentin, *Antisemitism* (New York: Viking Press, 1936).

7. Peter Schafer, *Judeophobia* (Cambridge, MA: Harvard University Press, 1997), 22.

8. M. Radin, *The Jews among the Greeks and the Romans* (New York: Arno Press, 1973).

9. Samuel Glassman, *Epic of Survival* (New York: Block Publishing Company, 1980), 4–5.

10. Joe Carmichael, *The Satanizing of the Jews* (New York: Fromm International Publishing Corporation, 1992), 47.

11. James Park, *Antisemitism* (London: Valentine & Mitchell, 1963), 62.

12. Robert Wistrich, *Antisemitism: The Long Hatred.* (London: Thames Methuen, 1991), 19.

13. Such as Hugo Valentin, Hannah Arendt, and Leon Poliakov.

14. James Caroll, *Constantine's Sword: The Church and the Jews* (Boston: Houghton Mifflin Co, 2001) and Julio Caro Baroja, *Los Judios en La Espana Moderna y contemporeana*, 2d ed (Madrid: Ed Istmo, 1978).

15. Blood was considered the carrier of hereditary characteristics. Pure blood meant one's ancestors had not mixed with undesirable persons (in this case Jewish).

16. Benzion Natanyahu, *The Origins of the Inquisition* (New York: Random House, 1995).

17. James Park, *The Conflict of the Church and the Synagogue* (New York: Athenum, 1981).

18. Samuel Glassman, *Epic of Survival:Twenty Five Centuries of Anti-Semitism* (New York: Block Publications Co, 1980), 61–62.

19. Wistrich, *Antisemitism, The Long Hatred*, 31.

20. Leon Poliakov, *From the Time of the Christ to Court Jews*, Volume 1 of *The History of Judaism* (New York: Vanguard Press, 1965), 67.

CHAPTER 2. SPAIN AND THE CONCEPT OF THE JEWISH RACE

1. "Marrano" will not be used in this book because it is an abusive term derived from the old Castilian word for pig. It originally may have been used by Jews to heap scorn on renegades who broke the prohibition against eating pork. Some writers use the word to describe converted Jews who secretly kept and practiced the Jewish faith.

2. Benzion Netanyahu, *The Origins of the Inquisition* (New York: Random House, 1995), 41.

3. Ibid., 42.

4. Ibid., 45.

5. At that time Spain was divided into three main areas: the Kingdom of Castile (which had recently incorporated the old Kingdom of Leon and the Muslim cities of Seville and Cordoba), the Kingdom of Aragon (which was enlarged in that century by the additions of Catalonia, Valenciona, and the Barbaric Islands), and Granada, the largest stronghold of the Muslims on the Iberian Peninsula.

6. See Leon Poliakov, *The History of Anti-Semitism* (New York: Vanguard Press, 1965–1975) II, 184; Jose Faur, *In the Shadow of History* (Albany: State University of New York Press, 1992), 29; Ellie Kedourie, *Spain and the Jews* (London: Thames and Hudson, 1992), 16; Netanayu, *The Origins of the Inquisition*, 3.

7. Erna Paris, *The End of the Days* (Amherst, NY: Prometheus Books), 171.

8. Ibid., 161.

9. In his *Book of Martyrs* (1570 edition), Fox uses this sense in English; or in a spiritual sense the "race of Satan" in Milton's *Paradise Lost* (1667).

10. Cited by M. Kayserling, "Un chansonnier marrane, Antoine de Montoro." *Revue Juive* 43, (1901): 263.

11. Solomon Ibn Verga, *Shever Yehuda*, sect 49. 1391. Published in Hebrew in Jerusalem. 1946.

12. Proceedings of the trial of La Guardia in Father F. Fita, *Torquemada et l'Inquisition.* (Paris, 1887), 17.

13. Anonymous. *Les Juifs en France.* Archives nationales K. 1710, No. 7.

14. Peggy Liss. *Isabel the Queen* (New York: Oxford University Press, 1992), 165, and Erna Paris, *End of Days*, 167.

15. Paris, *End of Days*, 170.

16. Ibid., 167.

17. Poliakov, *History of Anti-Semitism* II, 285.

18. Leon Poliakov, *Harvest of Hate* (Westport, CT: Greenwood Press, 1971), 59.

19. Paris, *End of Days*, 156.

20. Cecil Roth, *A History of the Marranos* (Philadelphia: Jewish Publication Society of America, 1932), 74.

21. Kedourie, *Spain and the Jews*, 48.

22. Paul Colongue, "Antisemitisme à l' époque Bismarkienne et l'attitude des Catholiques allemands." in *De l' antijudaisme à l'antisémitisme,* ed. Leon Poliakov (Lille: Université de Lille, 1969), 155.

23. Poliakov. *History of Anti-Semitism* II, 221; Cecil Roth, *The Spanish Inquisition* (New York: W.N. Norton, 1964), 197–207.

24. It is reported that Generals Patton and Eisenhower witnessed some evidence of torture when they entered the concentration camps of Ordhuff. See *Antisemitism in the Contemporary World,* ed. Michel Curtis (Boulder, CO: Westview Press, 1986), 32.

25. Spanish racism was much more widespread than just attitudes against the Jews. The Moriscos, descendants of converted Muslims, were also discriminated against in Spain, and so were the Indian-African-Spanish offspring in South America.

CHAPTER 3. SCIENCE AND THE CONCEPT OF THE JEWISH RACE

1. Pierre Bayle, *Traité de Tolérance Universelle* (Cambridge: Cambridge University Press, 2000), 137.

2. Charles Montesquieu, *Oeuvres Complètes* (Paris: N.A. Masson, Grasset, 1950–1955), vol. II, 262.

3. Jean-Jacques Rousseau, *Profession de foi du vicaire savoyard* (Paris: Hachette, 1912).

4. Cited in Leon Poliakov, *The Aryan Myth: A History of Racist and Nationalistic Ideas in Europe* (New York: Basic Books, 1974), 174–75.

5. Robert Wistrich, *Antisemitism* (London: Methuen, 1991), 44.

6. Robert Gran, *Les Oeuves Complètes de Voltaire,* (Paris: Mason, 1949), 152.

7. Poliakov, *History of Anti-Semitism III* (New York: Vanguard Press, 1965–75), 122.

8. Immanuel Kant professed a belief in the unity of mankind for philosophic reasons, but he was sure that the Jews were biologically different from non-Jews.

9. *A Voyage to Guinea in 1723*. Quoted in W. Jordan, *White over Black* (Chapel Hill: University of North Carolina Press, 1968), 17.

10. Count Stanislas de Clermont de Tonerre, a Revolutionary deputy reportedly to have said in the French Assembly: "The Jews should be denied everything as a nation, but granted everything as individuals." See John Efron, *Defenders of the Race* (New Haven: Yale University Press, 1994).

11. Richard Herrnstein and Charles Murray, *The Bell Curve: Intelligence and Class Structure in American Life* (New York: Free Press, 1994).

12. Stephen J. Gould, *The Mismeasure of Man* (New York: W. W. Norton, 1981), 73–112.

13. Leon Poliakov, *Hommes et Bêtes. Entretiens sur le racisme* (Paris: Mouton, 1975), 175. "The idea that sterility exists among human races finds an echo in every European language. The word mulatto is derived from the word mule, a sterile animal. Mulattoes until the 19th century were mistaken thought to be sterile, that is to say impotent or emasculated."

14. Attempts to classify Jews were made by Gaspard Lavater who admitted that he had lots of trouble in doing so and eventually gave up. See *L'art de connaitre les Hommes par la physionomie* (Paris, 1820), 168.

15. Although the Jews were never a race, Joseph Arthur de Gobineau (1816–82) and his British disciple, Houston Stewart Chamberlain (1855–1927), developed fantastic racial theories in which the "Western Aryans," people of India, became the Nordic and Germanic peoples of northern Europe and the Jews were an inferior race. These totally unfounded theories were adopted by the German Nazis who corrupted the word *Aryan* to mean Nordic, non-Semitic racially pure European. They also corrupted the swastika, an ancient Hindu religious symbol, into their own anti-Semitic symbol of race supremacy.

16. These languages include Zen, Armenian, Greek, Latin, Lithuanian, Slavonian, German, Celtic, English, French, Italian, and Spanish.

17. These languages include Arabic, Hebrew, Ethiopic, Amharic, and Amaric.

18. Julian Huxley, *Race in Europe* (London: Pamphlets on World Affairs, 1912).

19. Rudolph Virchow pointed out long ago that most Germans are not blond-haired and blue-eyed, as reported by Pat Shipman, in *The Evolution of Racism* (New York: Simon and Schuster, 1994).

20. John Beddoe, *On the Physical Characteristics of the Jews* (London: Transaction of the Ethnological Society of London, 1861), 222–37.

21. One of my Jewish students said that simply looking at a person he could tell whether he or she was Jewish or not. I told him to make a scientific experiment and record the data. He came back two weeks later and admitted that he had been wrong half the time.

22. John Efron, *Defenders of the Race*, 20–21.

23. The same explanation (climate) was given to me by one my cousins in 1995 to explain the origin of the "Negroes."

24. Johann Friedrich Blumenthal, *On the Natural Varieties of Mankind* (New York: Bergman Publishers, 1969).

25. Karl Rudolph, *Bertrage zur anthropologie*, cited by John Efron, *Defenders of the Race*, 21–26.

26. Richard Andre, *Zur Voksunde der Juden*, cited by John Efron, *Defenders of the Race*, 21–26.

27. William Frederick Edwards, letter to André Thierry about the latter's publication of *L'Histoire des Gaulois*, cited in Leon Poliakov, *The Aryan Myth*, 226.

28. The Dutch anatomist, Gregory Heinrich Wachter, wrote when noting the peculiarity "large nasal bone," and the "square chin" and the specifically Jewish impressions on both sides of the skull of a thirty-two year old Jewish man. "The cause of these impressions is that among the Jews, the muscles primarily used for talking and laughing are of a kind entirely different from those of Christians" (as reported in Efron's *Defenders of the Race*, 21).

29. Efron, *Defenders of the Race*, 42.

30. Gould, *The Mismeasure of Man*, 26.

31. J. F. Blumenbach, *Decas quarta collectionis suae cranorum diversarum gentium illustrata.* (Gottinghen, 1790), 10.

32. Poliakov, *The Aryan Myth*, 265.

33. R. C. Lewontin, Steven Rose, and Leon J. Kamin, *Not in Our Genes: Biology and Human Nature* (New York: Pantheon Books, 1984), 32.

34. William Z. Ripley, *The Races of Europe: A Sociological Study* (New York: Appleton and Co., 1899).

35. John Ingham, "Social Discrimination against the Jews, 1830–1930," in *Send These to Me: Jews and Other Immigrants in Urban America* (New York: Atheneum, 1975), 170–71.

36. Charles Davenport, *Heredity in Relation to Eugenics* (New York: Holt, 1911), 216.

37. Paul Popenhoe and Roswell Nill Johnson, *Applied Eugenics* (New York, 1938), 133.

38. Alfred C. Reed, "Immigration and Public Health," *Popular Science* (October 1913): 325.

39. Thomas Salmon, "Immigration and the Mixture of Races in Relation to the Mental Health of the Nation," in *The Modern Treatment of Nervous and Mental Health by American and British Authors*, eds. William A. White and Smith Ely Jeliffe (Philadelphia: Febiger, 1913), 258.

40. William Smith Ely and Henry L. Shiveley, "Immigration? A Factor in the Spread of Tuberculosis in New York City," *New York Medical Journal and Philadelphia Medical Journal* 77 (1903): 222–26.

41. Efron, *Defenders of the Race*, 199.

42. Claude Lévi-Strauss makes the same statement in "Race and History," in *The Race Question in Modern Science*, ed. UNESCO (New York: Columbia University Press, 1951), 74. According to Bernard Crick, "Such an effect is as dangerous as it is unneeded." See his foreword of Ivan Hannaford's *Race: The History of an Idea in the West* (Washington, DC: Woodrow Wilson Center Press, 1996).

43. John Efron, "Scientific Racism and the Mystique of Sephardic Racial Superiority," in *Leo Back Institute Yearbook* (New Haven: Yale University Press, 1993), 75–96.

44. Meyer Kayserling, "Sephardim," In vol. 11 of the *Jewish Encyclopedia* (New York: Funk and Wagnalls Co., 1901–5), 197.

45. Maurice Fishberg, *The Jews: A Study of Race and Environment* (New York: Charles Scribner's Sons, 1911).

46. As reported in Efron, *Defenders of the Race*, 23.

47. Ibid., 24.

48. Ibid., 91–122.

49. Ibid., 86.

50. Ibid., 85.

51. Adolph Neubauer, "Notes on the Race: Types of the Jews," *Journal of the Royal Anthropological Institute of Great Britain and Ireland*, 15 (1885): 19.

CHAPTER 4. THE FINAL SOLUTION

1. The French historian, Ernest Renan, who was a key figure in convincing his contemporaries that there was a Jewish race, had changed his mind by the end of the nineteenth century. The French encyclopedia of that period drew a sharp distinction between racial and ethnic groups. The anthropologist, Paul Topinard, put the matter clearly in *Elements of Anthropology:* "The Jews are only a religious federation, an ancient dispersed people, very mixed today at their origins. . . . From their beginnings . . . the Jews cannot be considered a race." Another anthropologist, Clémence Royer, the French translator of Darwin, denied the idea of a Jewish race before the Anthropological Society of Paris.

2. Arthur de Gobineau, "Essay on the Inequality of the Human Races, in *Gobineau. Selected Political Writings* ed. Michel D. Biddis (New York: Harper and Row, 1971).

3. Eugen Duhring, "The Jewish Question as a Question of Race, Morality and Culture with an Answer based on World History" in *"The Jewish Question" in German Literature,* ed. Ritchie Robertson (Oxford: Oxford University Press, 1999), 99.

4. Alex Bein, *The Jewish Question, Biography of a World Problem* (Madison, NJ: Fairleigh Dickinson University Press, 1990), 366.

5. Duhring, "The Jewish Question," 117, 157.

6. Bein, *The Jewish Question,* 20.

7. Paul Colongue. "L'antisémitisme à l'époque Bismarkienne et l'attitude des Catholiques allemands," in *De l'antijudaisme antique à l'antisémitisme contemporain,* ed. Valentin Nikiprowtzky (Lille: Presses Universitaires de Lille, 1977), 156.

8. Ibid., 171.

9. Robert S. Wistrich, *Antisemitism: The Longest Hatred* (London: Methuen, 1991), 63.

10. Ibid., 65.

11. Ibid., 129.

12. Ibid., 128.

13. Norman H. Bayes, *The Speeches of Adolph Hitler* (New York: Howard Fertig,1969), 740–41.

14. The murder of gypsies during World War II and the continued vilification and persecution of this group should put all the European host nations to shame.

15. John Roth and Michel Birenbaum, *Holocaust:Religious and Philosophical Implications* (New York: Paragon House, 1989), xiv.

16. Ibid., 94.

17. See Bernard Wasserstein, *Britain and the Jews of Europe, 1939–1945* (New York: Oxford University Press, 1988); Martin Gilbert, *Auschwitz and the Allies* (New York: Holt, Rinehart and Winston, 1981); David S. Wyman, *Abandonment of the Jews. America and the Holocaust. 1941–1945* (New York: Pantheon Books, 1984).

18. Wyman, *Abandonment of the Jews,* 395.

19. Alain F. Corcos, *The Little Yellow Train* (Tucson, AZ: Hats Off Books, 2004), 173.

20. Correspondence to the Dickstein Committee. Com.VI. Incoming Corres. File in Legis 17436.

21. *Christian Century,* 30 December 1942.

22. U.S. Department of State. *Foreign Relations of the United States,* Series VI, 1943, 143–44.

23. Willem Vissert Hooft, *Memoirs* (Philadelphia: Westminster Press, 1973), 167.

24. National Refuge Service papers No. 325, Minutes of Migration and Alien Status, May 11, 1943.

25. Gilbert: *Auschwitz and the Allies* (New York: Holt, Rinehart & Winston, 1985), 98.

26. Ibid., 133.

27. R. Sarraute and P. Tager. *Les Juifs sous l'occupation allemande. Recueil des textes officiels et allemands.* (Paris: Centre de Documentation Juive contemporaine, 1982), 18.

28. Richard Weisberg. *Vichy Law and the Holocaust in France* (New York: New York University Press 1996), 40.

29. Ibid.

30. R. Sarraute and P. G. Trager, *Les Juifs sous l'occupation allemande,* 185–92.

31. Weisberg, *Vichy Law,* 60–61.

32. Ibid., 384–85.

33. Michel Arbitol, *The Jews of North Africa during the Second World War* (Detroit, MI: Wayne State University Press, 1989), 63.

34. Doris Bensimon, *Les Grandes Raffles* (Paris: Edouard Privat., 1987), 65.

35. Corcos, *The Little Yellow Train.*

INTRODUCTION TO PART II

1. The words races, species, and genera were often confused. For example, in *Antisemitism and Jewish Uniqueness,* page 9, Arthur Hertzberg wrote: "In prosaic daily life, what Jews wanted to achieve was sufficient equality and likeness to others, to become species of the same genus as all individuals or groups." What he meant was to become members of the same species. He makes the same mistake on page 10.

2. Among those was John Ray (1627–1705), who went so far as to affirm that the difference between a white man and a black man is not greater than the one between a white cow and a black cow *(A Discourse on the Specific Differences of Plants, 1674;* cf. History of the Royal Society of London, III, 162–73).

Another was Johann Friedrich Blumenbach (1752–1840), who stated that the varieties of mankind, as accepted by various thinkers, seemed to have been arbitrarily chosen in regard to both numbers and definition (*On the Natural Varieties of Mankind* [London: Longman, Green, Roberts, & Green, 1865]).

3. I receive all kinds of letters from Jewish organizations which assume I am Jewish because many Corcos are Jewish. But I am not. Family names do not make people Jewish, Christian, Moslem, nor do they make them French, German, or American. A famous scientist, Gregor Mendel, is believed to have a Jewish name, but he was not Jewish; he was a Catholic priest and an abbot.

CHAPTER 5. THE MYTH OF HUMAN RACES

1. Alan Goodman, "Six Wrongs of Racial Science," in Curtis Stokes, Theresa Melendez, and Genice Rhodes-Reed, *Race in the 21st Century America* (East Lansing: Michigan State University Press, 2001), 44.

2. The fact remains that many Africans have wooly hair and dark skin. Likewise, many Asians have epicanthic folds, dry ear wax, and shoveled teeth. Why do these characteristics appear to be "linked?" In the past—and it is still true to some degree today—these populations were isolated, or semi-isolated, and were unlikely to come in contact and interbreed with populations that did not have their characteristics. As populations disperse and intermix, which is a tendency in the modern world, these "racial" traits will become less concentrated. This does not mean that the appearance of people will become uniform, rather that "racial" traits will less often be found together in the same individual.

3. Alain F. Corcos, *The Myth of Human Races* (East Lansing: Michigan State University Press, 1997), 193–99.

4. Ibid., 179–85.

5. R. Branda and J. Eaton, "Skin Color and Nutrient Photolysis. An Evolutionary Hypothesis." *Science* 201 (1978): 625–26.

6. Nina G. Jablonski and George Chaplin, "Skin Deep," *Scientific American* (October 2002): 75.

7. Frank Livingstone, "On the Non-existence of Human Races," *Current Anthropology* (June 1962): 278; Ashley Montagu, ed., *The Concept of Race* (London: Collier Macmillan, 1964); Margaret Mead, Theodosius Dobzhansky, Ethel Tobach, Robert Light, eds., *Science and the Concept of Race* (New York: Columbia University Press, 1968); Ashley Montagu, *Man's Most Dangerous Myth: The Fallacy of Race* (New York: Columbia University Press, 1968); Theodosius Dobzhansky, *Mankind Evolving* (New Haven: Yale University Press, 1962).

CHAPTER 6. JEWISH BLOOD, GENES, AND DISEASES

The epigraph to this chapter is cited in Leon Poliakov, *The Aryan Myth* (New York: Basic Books, 1974), 44.

1. Ashley Montagu, *Man's Most Dangerous Myth: The Fallacy of Race* (Cleveland: World Publishing Co., 1964), 226.

2. In *The Myth of the Jewish Race* (41, 54, 92, 116), Patai and Wing use "Jew-

ish blood" and "Jewish genes," sometimes in the same paragraph. In 1994 Stephen Katz wrote in *The Holocaust in Historical Context* (1, 100) "It was not Jewish numbers, but Jewish genes that mattered." In the same year, Norman Cantor wrote: "The Jews are superior intellectually, and as long as Jewish genes exist, the extraordinary impact Jews had in twentieth century thought will continue indefinitely" (*The Sacred Chain*, 423).

3. George L. Moss, *Toward the Final Solution. A History of European Racism* (New York: Howard Fertig, 1978), 29.

4. Corcos, *The Myth*, 163–65.

5. Among these are Juan Comas, "Racial Myths," in *The Race Question in Modern Science* (Paris, UNESCO, 1951); Amran Scheinfeld, *Your Heredity and Environment* (New York: Lippincott, 1965); and Ashley Montagu, *Human Heredity* (New York: Mentor Books, 1960).

6. A. E. Mourant, Ada C. Kopec, and Kazimiera Domaniewka-Sobczak, *The Genetics of the Jews*: (Oxford: Clarendon Press, 1978), Preface.

7. Raphael Patai and Jennifer Patai Wing, *The Myth of the Jewish Race* (New York: Charles Scribner's Sons, 1975), 245.

8. Batsheva Bonne-Tamir and Avoam Adam, *Genetic Diversity among Jews* (New York: Oxford University Press, 1992), 259 and 319.

9. Ibid., Prologue.

10. There are also no "Black" diseases. Sickle cell anemia, which has been called a "Black" disease, is found also in other human groups.

CHAPTER 7. THE JEWS

The epigraph to this chapter is drawn from Cecil Roth, *A History of the Marranos* (Philadephia: Hebrew Press of the Jewish Publication Society, 1932), 315.

1. Racists and anti-Semites are necessarily believers in biological determinism. It has been said that if the ideology had not existed at the time of Hitler, the Nazis would have had to invent it. See Richard Levontin, Stephen Rose, and Leon Kamrin, *Not in Our Genes* (New York: Pantheon Books, 1984), 17.

2. Richard Lewontin et al., *Not in Our Genes*, 268.

3. It was later discovered that Dolly's clone was aging prematurely. Such a discovery might lead to a better understanding of aging. See Paul G. Shiels et al., "Analysis of Telomere Lengths in Cloned Sheep," *Nature* 199 (1999): 316–17.

4. This myth is still believed by some school officials.

5. As defined by Richard Lewontin in his foreword to Richard Lerner's *Final Solutions* (University Park: Pennsylvania State University Press, 1992).

6. *Time*, March 10, 1986.

7. E. B. Tylor, "Evolution in Social Organization," in *Evolution and Anthropology: A Centennial Appraisal* (Washington, DC: Anthropological Society of Washington, 1959), 126–43.

8. Customs are sometimes responsible for acquired physical characteristics, but these characteristics are not hereditary. Among them are foot binding among Chinese women and circumcision among Jews and Muslims.

9. Our ability to use language depends on the structural characteristics of our throat and mouth, combined with what we learned through experience. The nervous and endocrine systems are of particular importance in setting behav-

ioral patterns which affect what we learn, and both of these systems are ultimately dependent on our genes.

10. Theodosius Dobzansky, *Mankind Evolving* (New Haven: Yale University Press, 1962), 59.

11. Cited in Alan Dershowitz, *The Vanishing American Jew* (Boston: Little, Brown & Co., 1997), 84.

12. The term "born Jewish" was used as late as 1997 by Alan Dershowitz in *The Vanishing American*, 84. It also can be found in books by authors who should know better: Calvin Langmuir in *History, Religion, and Antisemitism*, 238, wrote: "The patriarch of antisemitism [Wilhelm Marr] married two women, one who was half-Jewish ad one who was fully Jewish."

13. Endelman, *Radical Assimilation in English Jewish History, 1656–1945* (Bloomington: Indiana University Press, 1990), 82.

14. Dimmerstein, *Anti-Semitism in America*, 124.

15. The assumption that mitochondrial DNA is inherited only from the mother may not be correct. A report in *Science* (December 1999) casts doubt.

16. During the German occupation of France during World War II, a few individuals with Jewish names convinced the authorities they were not Jews and escaped death.

17. Robert Badinter, *Un antisémitisme ordinaire* (Paris: Fayard, 1977), 65.

18. Fernand Corcos, *Auto-reform* (New York: Editions de la Maison Française, 1945), 40.

Introduction to Part III

1. Historians write about Jews, who remain Jews, not about those who abandon Judaism.

Chapter 8. In the Beginning

1. To begin the history of the Jews so early is somewhat incorrect because there was not as yet a people of Israel unified by religion. Before that, these semi-nomadic wanderers had a religion similar to their neighbors: totemistic, animistic, and polytheistic. Only after the descendants of these wanderers settled in Palestine with their monotheistic religion in the late thirteenth century BCE did the history of the Jews begin.

2. Abraham Leon Sachar, *A History of the Jews* (New York: Alfred A. Knopf, 1966), 16.

3. Ibid., 36.

4. Cecil Roth, *A History of the Jews. From Earliest Times through the Six Day War* (New York: Schocken, 1970), 23.

5. Paul Goodman, *History of the Jews*. Revised and enlarged by Israel Cohen (New York: E. P. Dutton & Co., 1953), 29.

6. Avner Falk, *A Psychoanalytic History of the Jews* (Madison, NJ: Farleigh Dickinson University Press, 1996).

7. Ibid., 130.

8. Sachar, *History of the Jews*, 94.
9. Ibid., 95.
10. Ibid., 24.
11. Ibid., 79.
12. Roth, *History*, 66.
13. Sachar, *History*, 89.
14. Roth, *History*, 64.
15. Sachar, *History*, 88.
16. Ibid., 105.
17. Goodman, *History*, 42, and Cecil Roth, *History*, 81.
18. Falk, *A Psychoanalytic History*, 255.
19. Sachar, *History*, 111.
20. Archibald Sayce, *The Races of the Old Testament* (London: The Religious Tract Society Press, 1891).

Chapter 9. Jewish Proselytism

1. See Arthur Ruppin, "The Jewish Population in the World," in *The Jewish People, Past and Present* (New York: Henry Holt and Co., 1946); Salo W. Baron, *A Social History of the Jews*, 2nd ed. (Philadelphia: Jewish Pulication Society, 1952–1958); and A. Roudinesco, *Le malheur d' Israel* (Paris: Editions Cluny, 1956).
2. This is the opinion of Salomon Reinach expressed in his article, "Diaspora," *Jewish Encyclopedia* vol.4, 560–71. This is also the opinion of Ernest Renan, "Judaism: Race or Religion," *Contemporary Jewish Word* 6 (1883): 436–44.
3. Roman conversions explain why many Jews have common Italian names. See Max Margolis and Alexander Max, *The History of the Jewish People* (New York: Temple Books, 1974), 293.
4. Roudinesco, *Le malheur*, 3.
5. Ben Sasson, *A History of the Jewish People*, 2 vols. (Cambridge MA: Harvard University Press, 1976).
6. Roudinesco, *Le malheur*, 21.
7. Max Radin, *The Jewish People: The Jews among the Greeks and the Romans* (New York: Arno Press, 1973), 316.
8. Josephus Flavius, *Antiquitates Judiciae* (Grand Rapids, MI: Kregel Publications, 1988).
9. Margolis and Max, *History*, 290.
10. Leon Poliakov, vol. 1 of *The History of Anti-Semitism*. (New York: Vanguard Press, 1965–1985), 11.
11. Hugo Valentin, *Anti-Semitism* (New York: Viking Press, 1936), 25.
12. Cecil Roth, *A Short History of the Jews* (London: East and West Library, 1948), 143. Also see M. Fishberg, *The Jews. A Study of Race and Environment* (New York: Charles Scribner and Sons, 1911), 77.
13. Poliakov, vol. 2 of *History of Antisemitism*, 14.
14. Raphael Patai and Jennifer Patai Wing, *The Myth of the Jewish Race* (New York: Charles Scribner's Sons, 1975), 63.
15. Samuel Glassman, *Epic of Survival*, 48.

16. Patai and Wing, *The Myth of the Jewish Race*, 65.

17. Goodman, *History of the Jews*, 54.

18. Ben Zion Woholder, "The Halakak and the Proselytizing of Slaves during the Gaonic Era," *Historia Judaica* 13 (1956): 106.

19. André Chouraqui, *Les Juifs d'Afrique du Nord.* English translation. *Between East and West* (Philadelphia: Jewish Publication Society of America, 1968).

20. Richard Ayoun and Bernard Cohen, *Les Juifs d'Algérie, 2000 ans d'histoire* (Paris: Jean Claude Lattes, 1982), 36.

21. Jacob Oliel, *Les juifs du Sahara: Le Toutat au moyen age* (Paris: CNRS Editions, 1994), 8.

22. W. Baron, *A Social and Religious History of the Jewish People* (Philadelphia: Jewish Publication Society, 1937 and 1952–1958), 176.

23. Chouraqui, *Between East and West*, 11.

24. Ibid., 12.

25. Oliel, *Les Juifs*, 7.

26. Ibn Khaldum, *Histoire des Berbères et des dynasties musulmanes.* Slane translation. (Paris: P. Geuther, 1925)

27. Chouraqui, East and West, 19.

28. Ibid., 19

29. Tertian, *Ad notiones*, I. 3.

30. Ayoum, *Juifs d'Algérie*, 36.

31. Chouraqui, *Juifs d'Afrique du Nord*, 3.

32. A few years ago most of the Falashas emigrated to Israel.

33. David Kessler, *The Fallashas. The Forgotten Jews of Ethiopia* (London: George Allen & Unwin, 1982).

34. Tudor Parfit. *Journey to the Vanished City: The Search for a Lost Tribe of Israel* (New York: St. Martin's Press. 1992.

35. Steve Jones, *Y: The Descent of Men* (Boston: Houghton, Mifflin, 2003).

36. A similar study confirmed the oral tradition among the descendants of the slave Sally Hemmings that Thomas Jefferson was their ancestor.

37. Donald Leslie, *The Survival of the Chinese Jews: The Jewish Community of Kaifeng* (Leiden, The Netherlands: E. J. Brill, 1972), 2.

38. Abram Sachar, *A History of the Jews* (New York: Alfred A. Knopf, 1966), 251.

39. The manuscript is now in the library of the Hebrew Union College, Cincinnati. See Leslie, *Chinese Jews*, 5.

40. In the twentieth century a few fugitives from Russia and Nazi Europe settled in China but they did not remain there.

41. Leslie, *Chinese Jews*, 105.

42. Patricia Needle, *East Gate of the Kaifeng Jews: A Jewish World Inside China* (Minneapolis: University of Minnesota Press, 1985).

43. Wangzhi Gao, "The Assimilation of the Chinese Jews," in Patricia Needle, ed., *Kaifeng*, 238.

44. Michael Pollack, "Early History of the Kaifeng Jews," in Patricia Needle, ed. *Kaifeng*, 125.

45. T. V. Parasuram, *India's Jewish Heritage* (New Delhi: Sagar Publications, 1982).

46. If a "white" rabbi entered a "black" synagogue, the dark-skinned rabbi

had to stand back and let him perform divine service. See J. B. Segal, *A History of the Jews of Cochin* (London: Valentine Mitchell & Co,1981), 53.

47. Ibid., 75.

48. Ibid., 13.

49. Another hypothesis is that they came to India in the sixth century, in flight from religious persecution in Southern Arabia.

50. Joan G. Roland, *Jews in British India* (Waltham, MA: Brandeis University Press, 1969), 12.

51. Ezekiel, Barber, *The Bene Israel of India* (Washington, DC: University Press of America, 1981), 13.

52. Roland, *Jews in British India*, 12.

53. King Solomon may have had one or more princesses from India in his harem.

54. Barber, *The Bene Israel*, 21.

55. Roland, *Jews in British India*, 16.

56. Ibid., 69.

57. Parasuram, *India's Jewish Heritage*, 58. Ibid., 94.

59. Ibid., 103.

60. Nathan Katz and Ellen S. Goldberg, *The Last Jews of Cochin: Jewish Identity in Hindu India* (Columbia: University of South Carolina Press, 1993), 284.

61. D. M. Dunlop, *The History of the Jewish Kazars* (New York: Shocken Books,1967), 8.

62. That was the process in the Kingdom of Adiabene in the first century CE and Yemen in the fifth century CE. See S. Baron, *A Social History of the Jews* (Philadelphia: Jewish Publication Society, 1937, 1952–1958), and K. K. Hitti, *History of the Arabs*, 6th ed. (London and New York: New York University Press, 1961), 60–62.

63. Solomom Grazel, *A History of the Jews: From the Babylonian Exile to the Present* (New York: New English Library, 1968).

64. Norman Golb and Omeljan Pristak, *Khazarian Hebrew Documents of the Tenth Century* (Ithaca: Cornell University Press, 1982).

65. Arthur Koestler, *The Thirteen Tribes*, 17: "[Because] the large majority of surviving Jews in the world is of Eastern Europe and [if many are of Khazar origin] this would mean that their ancestors came not from the Jordan, but from the Caucasus, once believed to be the cradle of the *Aryan Race* [italics mine], and that genetically they are more closely related to the Hun, Ulgur, and Magyar tribes than the seed of Abraham, Isaac and Jacob. Should this turn out to be the case, the term anti-Semitism would become void of meaning, based on a misapprehension shared by the killers and their victims. The story of the Khazar Empire as it slowly emerges from the past looks like the most cruel hoax which history has ever perpetuated."

66. Dunlop, *Jewish Kazars*, 96.

CHAPTER 10. DARKNESS AT NOON

1. The Dark Ages were so named because civilization in Europe had taken a step backwards. Historians now use the terms early, middle, and late to re-

---

flect the fact that, in other parts of the world, civilization was still slowly progressing. Unfortunately, most Europeans lived in such miserable conditions for several centuries after the fall of Rome that these unhappy times indeed merit the name of Dark Ages.

2. Bert Engelmann, *Germany without Jews* (New York: Bantam Books, 1984), 5.

3. I am referring to the current French, Italian, and Spanish territories which are the result of various unifications.

4. Emily Taitz, *The Jews of Medieval France* (Westport, CT: Greenwood Press, 1994), 24.

5. Shlomo Deschen and Walter P. Zenner, *Jewish Societies in the Middle East: Community, Culture, and Authority* (New York: University Press of America, 1982), 169.

6. Patai and Wing, *Myth of the Jewish Race*, 130.

7. Bernard Blumenkranz, *Histoire des Juifs de France* (Toulouse: Collection Judaica, Edouard Privat, 1972), 49.

8. Annie Perchenet, *Histoire des Juifs de France* (Paris: Les éditions du Cerf, 1988), 29.

9. Patai and Wing, *Myth of the Jewish Race*, 104–6.

10. Poliakov, vol. 1 of *History of Antisemitism*, 36.

11. Ibid.

12. Bernard Blumenkrantz, "The Roman Church and the Jews," in Roth, *The World History*, 86–96. See also T. Reinach, "Agobard et les juifs," *Revue des Études Juives* 50 (1950).

13. Armand Lunel, *Juifs de Provence, Languedoc et les Etats Français du Pape* (Paris: Albin Michel, 1975), 9.

14. Ibid.

15. Michel Rouche. "Les baptêmes forcés des Juifs en Gaule Merovingienne," in *L'antijudaisme antique a l'antisemtisme contemporain*, ed. Valentin Nikiprowtsky (Lille: Presses Universitaires de Lille, 1975).

16. Taitz, *Jews of Medieval France*, 52.

17. Ibid., 175.

18. *Chronique de Michel le Syrien*, in Blumenkrantz, *Histoire des Juifs de France* (Toulouse: Edouard Privat), 18.

19. Leon Poliakov, vol. 1, *History of Antisemitism*, 34.

20. Vercingetorix, (d.46 BCE), Gallic king who resisted Julius Cesar in revolt of 52 BCE, was ultimately defeated and put to death.

CHAPTER 11. GHETTO LIFE

1. Todd Endelman, *Radical Assimilation in English Jewish History, 1651–1945* (Bloomington: Indiana University Press, 1990), 9.

2. Frances Malino, *The Sephardic Jews of Bordeaux* (Tuscaloosa: The University of Alabama Press, 1978), 5.

3. Ibid., 11.

4. For a description of life in the ghetto, see Roth, *A History of the Jews*, 273–94.

5. Sachar, *A History of the Jews*, 234.

6. Margolis and Max, *A History of the Jewish People*, 531.

7. About two million Russian Jewish immigrants came to the United States.

8. Paul Johnson, *A History of the Jews* (New York: Harper and Row, 1987), 358–63.

9. Today, many of the genes for these deleterious diseases can be detected by sophisticated tests and future parents may receive counseling.

CHAPTER 12. LIBERTY, EQUALITY, AND FRATERNITY?

1. A. Schwarfuchs, *Les Juifs de France* (Paris: Albin-Michel, 1975), 205.

2. Francis Malino, *The Sephardic Jews of Bordeaux, Assimilation and Emancipation in Revolutionary France* (Tuscaloosa: University of Alabama Press, 1978), 1.

3. The Rights of Man affirmed that all citizens of France were born free and equal. Because the Jews were not citizens of France, having always been considered foreigners, another step had to be taken for them to be free. Adrien Duport, a jurist and deputy of Paris, supported by the Parisian nobility and Condorcet, the philosopher turned politician, favorably influenced the majority of the French Assembly. On September 21, 1791, Duport proposed a law to make citizens of all the Jews residing in France, which passed despite some opposition.

4. Guido de Ruggiero, *The History of European Liberalism* (London: Oxford University Press, 1959).

5. Raphael Mahler, *A History of Modern Jewry, 1780–1815* (London: Valentine, Mitchell, 1971), 32.

6. Todd Endleman, "German Jews in Victorian England," in eds. Jonathan Frankel and Steve Zipperstein *Assimilation and Community: The Jews in Nineteenth-Century Europe* (Cambridge: Cambridge University Press, 1992), 71.

7. J. H. Kievale, "The Social Vision of Bohemian Jews: Intellectuals and Community in the 1840s," in *Assimilation and Community*, 247, and Michael Siber, "The Entrance into the Hungarian Society in the 1840s," in *Assimilation and Community*, 308.

8. Emile Marmostein, *Haven at Bay: The Jewish Kulturkamp on the Holy Land*, cited by Paul Johnson, *History of the Jews* (New York: Harper and Row, 1987), 312.

9. Ibid.

10. C. Piette-Samson, *Les Juifs de Paris, 1808–1840; problèmes d'acculturation* (Paris: Dalloz, 1973), 283.

11. Leon Kahn estimates about 66 intermarriages per year from a total of 250 Jewish marriages per year, cited by Phyllis Cohen Albert, *The Modernization of French Jewry: Consistory and Community in the Nineteenth Century*, 19.

12. Galvin Goldscheider and Alan Zuckerman, *Transformation of the Jews*, 225.

13. Ibid.

14. Patai, *The Myth of the Jewish Race*, 115.

15. Ibid.

16. Goldscheimer and Zuckerman, *The Transformation of the Jews*, 91.

17. Uriah Zevi Engleman, *The Rise of the Jews in the Western World* (New York: Arno Press, 1973), 190–201.

18. Patai and Patai, *The Myth of the Jewish Race*, 82.

19. Zollchan, *Are the Jews a Race?*, 478.

20. T. M. Endleman, "The Englishness of Jewish Modernity in England," in J. Katz, ed., *Toward Modernity: The European Jewish Model* (New Brunswick, NJ: Rutgers University Press, 1987), 225–26.

21. T. M. Endleman, *Radical Assimilation in English Jewish History 1656–1945* (Bloomington: Indiana University Press, 1995), 3.

22. Albert Hyamson, *A History of the Jews in England* (London: Methuen, 1928), 37.

23. Evron Boas, *Jewish State or Israeli Nation* (Bloomington: Indiana University Press, 1995), 57.

24. For a detailed study of this thesis see Todd Endleman, *Radical Assimilation in English Jewish History 1656–1945.*

25. Endleman, *Radical Assimilation*, 17 and 33.

26. Nora Levin, *The Jews in the Soviet Union since 1917: Paradox of Survival* (New York: New York University Press,1988), 266–67.

CHAPTER 13. JEWS IN THE UNITED STATES

The epigraph to this chapter is cited by Ellen Jaffe McClain in *Embracing the Stranger: Intermarriage and the Future of the American Jewish Community* (New York: Basic Books, 1995), 15.

1. *New York Times*, 7 June 1991, p. 8S. See also Debra Nussbaum Cohen, "Comprehensive New Survey Found most American Jews Intermarry," *Arizona Jewish Post* 21 June 1991, 1 and 2.

2. Samuel C. Hellman, *Portrait of American Jews* (Seattle: University of Washington Press, 1995), 5.

3. Eli Faber, *A Time for Planting. The First Migration: 1654–1820.* vol. 1 of *The Jewish People in America* (Baltimore: Johns Hopkins University Press, 1992), 1.

4. Anita Libman Lebenson, *Jewish Pioneers* (New York: Brentano's, 1931), 854.

5. Macolm Stern, "The Function of Genealogy in American Jewish History," in *Essays in American Jewish History to Commemorate the Tenth Anniversary of Founding the American Jewish Archives*, under the direction of Jacob Rader Marcus (Cincinnati, OH: American Jewish Archives 1958), 63–86, 94–97.

6. Jews undoubtedly had sexual relations with their female slaves, and raised the children of such unions as Jews. Some are said to be the ancestors of the "Black" Jews of Harlem.

7. Paul Johnson, *A History of the Jews* (New York: Harper and Row), 310.

8. Hashia R. Diner, *"A Time for Gathering: The Second Migration, 1820–1880*, vol. 2 of *The Jewish People in America*, 139.

9. Henry Feingold, *A Time for Searching. Entering Mainstream*, vol. 4 of *The Jewish People in America* (Baltimore: Johns Hopkins University Press, 1992), 42.

10. Ibid., 87.

11. Leonard Dinnerstein, *Antisemitism in America* (New York: Oxford University Press, 1994), 241.

12. Robert Gordis, *Judaism in a Christian World* (New York: McGraw-Hill, 1966), 186.

13. Heillman, *Portraits of American Jews*, 74.

CHAPTER 14. A SUMMARY

1. Ashley Montagu, *Man's Most Dangerous Myth: The Fallacy of Race* (Cleveland: World Publishing Company, 1964), 329.

2. Raphael Patai and Jennifer Patai Wing, *The Myth of the Jewish Race* (New York, Charles Scribner's Sons, 1975), 272–82.

3. A. E. Mourant, "The Blood Group of the Jews," *Jewish Journal of Sociology* 1 (1959): 155–75.

4. Only by mating similar phenotypes can we maintain the breeds of dogs, cattle, horses, sheep, and other domestic animals.

5. When the author was in the French Air Force in Morocco during World War II, he met a soldier with a common French name who was writing to his mother in Polish. Asked why, he explained that his great-grandfather had been a soldier in Napoleon's army who married a Polish girl and never returned to France.

6. Basheva Bonné-Tamir and Avinoam Adam, eds., *Genetic Diversity among Jews, Diseases and Markers at the DNA Level* (New York: Oxford University Press, 1992), 305.

7. Richard Goodman, *Genetic Disorders among the Jewish People* (Baltimore: Johns Hopkins University Press, 1979), 29.

8. For a definition and the use of this statistic tool, see L. L. Cavalli-Shorza and W. F. Bodmer, *Genetics of Human Populations* (San Francisco: W. H. Freeman, 1971) and A. Jacquard, *The Genetic Structure of Population Genetics* (New York: Springer-Verlag, 1974).

9. See the preface to Batsheva Bonné-Tamir and Avinoam Adam, eds., *Genetic Diversity among Jews*.

10. Bonné-Tamir and Avinoam Adam, eds. *Genetic Diversity among Jews* 38.

11. The most recent estimate.

CONCLUSION

1. A reason seldom stressed is that Jewish parents did not want their children exposed to the psychological and often physical damage of anti-Semitism.

2. Cited in Evron, *The Jewish State or Israeli Nation*, 71.

3. As reported by Luc Ferry, "Qu'est ce qu'être juif," *Le Point*, 12 (October 1999), 92.

4. Dershowitz, *The Vanishing American Jew*, 3.

5. Simon Rawidowicz, *Israel: The Ever Dying People* (Madison, NJ: Fairleigh Dickinson University Press, 1986).

6. Norman Cantor, *The Sacred Chain: The History of the Jews* (New York: Harper and Collins, 1994).

7. Michael Curtis, *Antisemitism in the Contemporary World* (Boulder, CO: Westview Press, 1986).

8. Pierre Birnbaum, *Jewish Destinies* (New York: Hill and Wang, 2000), 56.

9. Norman Cantor, *The Sacred Chain*, 334.

10. Dominique Schaffer, "Perceptions of Antisemitism in France," in *Antisemitism in the Contemporary World*.

11. Wendy Stallard Flory, "The Psychology of Antisemitism," in *Antisemitism in the Contemporary World*, 244.

Selected Bibliography

Abel, Ernest. *The Roots of Anti-Semitism.* Madison, NJ: Farleigh Dickinson University Press, 1975.

Abitol, Michael. *The Jews of North Africa During the Second World War.* Detroit, MI: Wayne State University Press, 1989.

Abrahams, Israel. *Jewish Life in the Middle Ages.* Philadelphia: Jewish Publication Society, 1920.

Albright, W. F. *From Stone Age to Christianity.* Baltimore, MD: Johns Hopkins University Press, 1946.

Anti-Deflamation League. *Antisemitism Worldwide.* Tel Aviv: Tel Aviv University Press, 1997.

Aubery, Pierre. *Milieux Juifs de la France Contemporaine.* Paris: Librairie Plomb, 1957.

Ayoun, Richard, and Bernard Cohen. *Les Juifs d' Algérie: 2000 ans d'histoire.* Paris: Jean Claude Lattes, 1982.

Azoulay, Katja Gibel. *Black, Jewish, and Interracial Marriage.* Durham, NC: Duke University Press, 1997.

Badinter, Robert. *Un antisémitisme ordinaire: Vichy et les avocats juifs (1940–44).* Paris: Fayard, 1997.

Banton, Michael, and Johnathan Hardwood. *The Race Concept.* New York: Prager Publishers, 1975.

Barber, Ezekiel. *The Bene-Israel of India.* Washington, DC: University Press of America, 1981.

Baron, S. W. *Ancient and Medieval Jewish History.* New Brunswick, NJ: Rutgers University Press, 1972.

———. *A Social and Religious History of the Jewish People.* Philadelphia: Jewish Publication Society, 1937 and 1952–1958.

Barzun, Jacques. *Race: A Study in Modern Superstition.* New York: Harcourt Brace, 1937.

Beek, M. A. *A Short History of Israel.* London: Hodder and Stoghton, 1957.

Bein, Alex. *The Jewish Question, Biography of a Problem.* Madison, NJ: Fairleigh Dickinson University Press, 1990.

Benayoun, Chantal. *Les Juifs et la politique.* Paris: Editions du CNRS, 1984.

Berger, David. *History and Hate: The Dimensions of Anti-Semitism.* Philadelphia: Jewish Publication Society, 1986.

Berger, Elmer. *The Jewish Dilemma.* New York: Devin-Adair Co., 1945.

157

Berkovitz, Jay. *The Shaping of Jewish Identity in 19th century France*. Detroit, MI: Wayne State University Press, 1989.

Beschloss, Michael. *The Conquerors: Roosevelt and Truman and the Destruction of Hitler's Germany*. New York: Simon and Schuster, 2002.

Birnbaum, Pierre. *Anti-Semitism in France: A Political History from Léon Blum to the Present*. Oxford and Cambridge: Blackwell, 1992.

——. *Histoire politique des Juifs de France; Entre l'universalisme et particularisme*. Paris: Presses de la Fondation Nationale des Sciences Politiques, 1990.

——. *Un mythe politique: La République Juive. De Léon Blum à Pierre Mendès-France*. Paris: Fayard, 1988.

Black, William Harman. *If I were a Jew*. New York: Real Book Company, 1938.

Blum, Harold. "Does the Melanin Pigment of Human Skin Have Adaptive Value?" *Quarterly Review of Biology* 3 (1961): 50–63.

Blumenkrantz, Bernard. *Histoire des Juifs de France*. Toulouse: Collection Franco-Judaica, Edouard Privat, 1972.

Bonné-Tamir, Batsheva, and Avinoam Adam, eds. *Genetic Diversity among Jews*. New York: Oxford University Press, 1992.

Bram, Joseph. "The Social Identity of the Jews." *Transaction of New York Academy of Sciences, ser. 2, VI* (1944).

Bright, John. *A History of Israel*, 3rd ed. Philadelphia, PA: Westminster Press, 1981.

Brown, Michael. *The Search for Eve*. New York: Harper and Row, 1990.

Burman, Edward. *The Inquisition: The Hammer of Heresy*. Wellinborough, Northampshire, UK: Aquarian Press, 1984.

Cantor, Norman. *The Sacred Chain: The History of the Jews*. New York: Harper Collins Publishers, 1994.

Carmichael, Joel. *The Satanizing of the Jews: Origin and Development of Mystical Anti-Semitism*. New York: Fromm International Publishing Corp., 1992.

Carroll, James. *Constantine's Sword. The Church and The Jews*. New York: Houghton Miffin, 2001.

Castro, Adolpho de, *The History of the Jews in Spain. From the Time of their Settlement in that Country till the Commencement of the Present Century* (Cadiz, 1847). Translated by Edward D. G. M. Kirwan. Westport, CT: Greenwood Press, 1972.

Cavalli-Sforza, L. L., and W. D. Bodmer. *Genetics of Human Populations*. San Francisco: W. H. Freeman, 1971.

Chazan, Robert. *Medieval Jewry in Northern France: A Political and Social History*. Baltimore, MD: The Johns Hopkins University Press, 1973.

Chouraqui, André. *Les Juifs d'Afrique du Nord*. Paris: Presses Universitaires de France, 1952. Translation as *Between East and West: A History of the Jews of North Africa*. Translated by Michel M. Bernet. Philadelphia: The Jewish Publication of Society of America, 1968.

Cohn-Sherbok, Dan. *The Crucified Jew. Twenty Centuries of Christian Anti-Semitism*. London: Harper-Collins, 1992.

Comay, Joan, *The Hebrew Kings*. London: Weidenfeld and Nicolson, 1976.

Conzelman, Hans. *Gentiles, Jews, Christians Polemics and Apologetics in the Greco-Roman Era*. Minneapolis, MN: Fortress Press, 1981.

Coote, Robert B., and Keith W. Whiteman. *The Emergence of Early Israel*. Sheffield, UK: Almond Press, 1987.

Corcos, Alain. *The Little Yellow Train: Survival and Escape from France, 1940–1944*. Tucson, AZ: Hats Off Books, 2004.

———. *The Myth of Human Races*. East Lansing: Michigan State University Press, 1997.

Curtis, Michael. *Antisemitism in the Contemporary World*. Boulder, CO: Westview Press, 1986.

Cutler, Allan Harris, and Ellen Elmquist Cutler. *The Jew as Ally of the Muslim*. Notre Dame, IN: University of Notre Dame Press, 1986.

Dawidowitz, Lucy. *The War against the Jews. 1933–1945*. New York: Holt, Rinehart, and Winston, 1975.

De Haas, Jacob. *History of Palestine: The Last Two Thousand Years*. New York: McMillan, 1934.

Delacampagne, Christian. *L'invention du racisme. Antiquité et moyen age*. Paris: Fayard, 1983.

De Lange, N. R. "The Origins of Anti-Semitism: Ancient Evidence and Modern Interpretation." In *Anti-Semitism in Instances of Crisis*, Sander L. Gillman and Stephen Katz, eds. New York: New York University Press, 1991), 21–37.

Dershowitz, Alan M. *The Vanishing American Jew: In the Search of Jewish Identity*. New York: Little Brown and Co., 1997.

Diaz-Mas, Paloma. *Sephardim: The Jews from Spain*. Chicago: University of Chicago Press, 1992.

Dinnerstein, Leonard. *Anti-Semitism in America*. New York: Oxford University Press, 1994.

Dippel, John Van Houten. *Bound upon a Wheel of Fire: Why so many German Jews made the Tragic Decision to Remain in Nazi Germany*. New York: Basic Books, 1996.

Dobzhansky, Theodosius. "The Race Concept in Biology." *The Scientific Monthly* 52 (1941): 165–67.

———. *Mankind Evolving*. New Haven: Yale University Press, 1962.

Dunlop, Douglas. *The History of the Jewish Khazars*. New York: Schoeken Books, 1967.

Edgar, Black. "Why Skin Comes in Colors." *California Wild* 53, no. 1 (Winter 2000): 6–7.

Efron, John. *Defenders of the Race: Jewish Doctors and Race Science in Fin de Siècle Europe*. New Haven: Yale University Press, 1994.

———. "Scientific Racism and the Mystique of Sephardic Racial Superiority." *Leo Back Institute Yearbook*, 1993.

Endelman, Todd M. *Radical Assimilation in English Jewish History 1656–1945*. Bloomington: Indiana University Press, 1990.

Englander, David. *The Jewish Enigma: An Enduring People.* New York: George Braziller, 1992.

Epstein, Simon. *L'antisémitisme français: aujourd'hui et demain.* Paris: Pierre Belmond, 1983.

Estel, L. "Race as an Evolutionary Concept." *American Journal of Physical Anthropology* 14 (1956): 378.

Evron, Boas. *The Jewish State or Israeli Nation.* Bloomington: Indiana University Press, 1995.

Falk, Avner. *A Psychoanalytic History of the Jews.* Madison, NJ: Farleigh Dickinson University Press, 1996.

Faur, Jose. *In the Shadow of History: Jews and Conversos at the Dawn of Modernity.* Albany: University of New York Press, 1992.

Fein, Helen. *The Persisting Question: Sociological Perspectives and Social Contexts of Modern Anti-Semitism.* Berlin: Walter de Gruyter, 1987.

Feingold, Henry. *The Jewish People in America.* Baltimore: Johns Hopkins University Press, 1992.

Finn, James. *The Jews of China.* Tapei: Ch'eng Wen Publishing Company, 1971.

Fishberg, Maurice. *The Jews. A Study of Race and Environment.* New York: Charles Scribner & Sons, 1911.

Frankel, Jonathan, and Stephen J. Zipperstein. *Assimilation and Community: The Jews in Ninteenth-Century Europe.* New York: Cambridge University Press, 1992.

Friedlander, Saul. *L'antisémitisme Nazi: Histoire d'une psychose collective.* Paris: Editions du Seuil, 1971.

———. *Nazi Germany and the Jews: The Years of Persecution.* New York: Harper Collins, 1997.

Gabba, E. "The Growth of anti-Judaism or the Greek Attitude towards Jews." In *The Cambridge History of Judaism.* Edited by W. D. Davies and L. Finkelstein. Vol. 2, *The Hellenistic Age* (Cambridge: Cambridge University Press, 1989), 614–56.

Gager, John. *The Origins of Anti-Semitism: Attitudes towards Judaism in Pagan and Christian Antiquity.* New York: Oxford University Press, 1985.

Gampel, Benjamin. *The Last Jews on Iberian Soil: Navarese Jewry 1479–1498.* Berkeley: University of California Press, 1988.

Gerber, David. *Anti-Semitism in American History.* Urbana: University of Illinois Press, 1986.

Gerber, Jane. *The Jews of Spain: A History of the Sephardic Jews.* New York: The Free Press, 1992.

Gilbert, Martin. *The Holocaust: A History of the Jews of Europe during the Second World War.* New York: Holt, Rinehart & Winston, 1985.

Gillman, Sander, and Stephen Katz, eds. *Anti-Semitism in the Period of Crisis.* New York: New York University Press, 1991.

Gilman, Stephen, and Edmund King. *An Idea of History: Selected Essays of Americo Castro.* Columbus: Ohio State University Press, 1977.

Ginio, Alisa Meyunas. *Jews Christians, and Muslims in the Mediterranean World after 1492.* Portland, OR: International Specialized Book Service, 1992.

Ginsberg, Benjamin. *The Fatal Embrace. Jews and the State: The Politics of Anti-Semitism.* Chicago: University of Chicago Press, 1993.

Gitlitz, David. *Secrecy and Deceit: The Religion of the Crypto-Jews.* Philadelphia: Jewish Publication Society, 1996.

Glassman, Samuel. *Epic of Survival: Twenty Five Centuries of Anti-Semitism.* New York: Block Publishing Company, 1980.

Golb, Norman, and Omlejean Pritsak. *Khazarian Hebrew Documents of the Tenth Century.* Ithaca: Cornell University Press, 1982.

Goldblatt, David. *Is the Jewish Race Pure? A Scientific Explanation.* New York: Goldblatt Publishing Company, 1933.

Golden, Peter. *Khazar Studies: An Historico-Philological Inquiry into the Origins of the Khazars.* Budapest: Akademiai Kiado, 1980.

Goldscheider, Calvin, and Allan Zuckerman. *The Transformation of the Jews.* Chicago: University Chicago Press, 1984.

Goodman, Alan. "Six Wrongs of Racial Science." In Stokes, Curtis, Theresa Melendez, and Genice Rhodes-Reed, eds. *Race in the Twenty-First Century America.* East Lansing: Michigan State University Press, 2001, 25–47.

Goodman, Paul. *History of the Jews.* New York: E. P. Dutton & Co., 1953.

Goodman, Richard M. *Genetic Disorders among the Jewish People.* Baltimore, MD: Johns Hopkins University Press, 1979.

Gould, Stephen. *The Mismeasure of Man.* New York: W. W. Norton, 1981.

Graeber, Jacque, and Stuart Britt, eds. *Jews in a Gentile World.* New York: Macmillan, 1942.

Grant, M. *The Jews in the Roman World.* New York: Scribner, 1973.

Grayzel, S. *The Church and the Jews in the Thirteenth Century, 1254–1314.* Detroit, MI: Wayne State University Press, 1966.

———. *A History of the Jews.* Philadelphia: Jewish Publication Society, 1947.

Greenberg, Gary. *The Moses Mystery: The African Origins of the Jewish People.* Secaucus, NJ: Carol Publishing House, 1997.

Grosser, Paul, and Edwin G. Halperin. *Anti-Semitism: Causes and Effects.* New York: Philosophical Library, 1983.

Guinebert, Charles. *Le monde juif vers le temps de Jésus.* New York: University Books, 1959.

Halcizer, Stephen. *Inquisition and Society in Early Modern Europe.* Totowa, NJ: Barnes and Noble, 1987.

Hannaford, Ivan. *Race, the History of an Idea in the West.* Washington, DC: Woodrow Wilson Center Press, 1996.

Hay, Malcolm. *The Foot of Pride: The Pressure of Christendom on the People of Israel for 1900 Years.* Boston: Beacon Press, 1950.

———. *Inquisition and Society in the Kingdom of Valencia, 1478–1834.* Berkeley: University of California Press, 1990.

Heiman, Samuel. *Portrait of American Jews: The Last Half of the Twentieth Century.* Seattle: University of Washington Press, 1994.

Hertzberg, Arthur. "Antisemitism and Jewish Uniqueness, Ancient and Contemporary." Syracuse, NY: Syracuse University Press, 1975. (April 1973).

———. *The Jews in America. Four Centuries of an Uneasy Encounter: A History.* New York: Simon and Schuster, 1989.

Hertzberg, Arthur, and Aron Hirt-Manheimer. *Jews: The Essence and Character of a People.* San Francisco: Harper, 1997.

Hillel, Marc. *Au nom de la race.* Paris: Fayard, 1975.

Hyman, Paula. *The Jews of Modern France.* Berkeley: University of California Press, 1998.

Huxley, Julian. *Race in Europe.* New York: Farrar and Rinehart, Inc., 1939.

Huxley, Julian, and Alfred Haddon. *We Europeans.* New York: Collier, 1936.

Isaac, Jules. *Genèse de l'antisémitisme.* Paris: Calmann-Levy, 1956.

Israel, Benjamin. *The Jews of India.* New Delhi: The Centre for Jewish and Interfaith Studies, Jewish Welfare Association, 1982.

Jablonski, Nina G., and George Chaplin. "The Evolution of Human Skin Coloration." *Journal of Human Evolution* 39, no.1 (1 July 2000): 57–106.

———. "Skin deep." *Scientific American* 228 (October 2002): 74.

Japheth, Maurice. *The Jews of India: A Brief Survey.* Bombay, May 1969.

Johnson, Paul. *A History of the Jews.* New York: Harper and Row, 1987.

Jordan, William Chester. *The French Monarchy and the Jews: From Philip Agustus to the Last Capetians.* Philadelphia: University of Pennsylvania Press, 1989.

Josephus Flavius. *The Essential Writings: A Condensation of Jewish Antiquities and The Jewish War.* Translated and edited by Paul L. Maier. Grand Rapids, MI: Kregel Publications, 1988.

Juster, J. *Les Juifs dans l'empire romain.* Paris: Guenther, 1914.

Kahn, Lothar. *Mirrors of the Jewish Mind.* New York: Thomas Yoseloff amd A. S. Barnes, 1968.

Kamen, Henry. *The Spanish Inquisition: A Historical Revision.* Bloomington: Indiana University Press, 1985.

Kaplan, Steven. *The Beta Israel (Falasha) in Ethiopia: From Earliest Times to the Twentieth Century.* New York: New York University Press, 1992.

Katz, Jacob. *From Prejudice to Destruction.* Cambridge, MA: Harvard University Press, 1980.

Katz, Nathan. *The Last Jews of Cochin.* Columbia: University of South Carolina Press, 1993.

———. *Studies of Indian Jewish Identity.* New Delhi: Manohar, 1995.

Katz, Steven. *The Holocaust in Historical Context.* New York: Oxford University Press,1994.

Kautsky, Karl. *Are the Jews a Race?* New York: International Publishers, 1926; republished by Greenwood Press, Westport, CT, 1972.

Kedourie, Ellie. *Spain and the Jews: The Sephardic Experience 1492 and After.* New York: Thames and Hudson, 1992.

Keimowitz, Hazel Kahn, and Wolfgang Mieder. *The Jewish Experience of Euro-*

pean Anti-Semitism. Burlington: Harry Khan Memorial Lectures, The Center for Holocaust Studies at the University of Vermont, 1995.

Kertzer, David J. *The Popes against the Jews*. New York: Vintage Books, 2002.

Kessler, David. *The Falashas*. London, Boston, Sydney: George Allen & Unwin, 1982.

Kingston, Paul. *Anti-Semitism in France during the 1930s: Organizations, Personalities and Propaganda*. Hull, UK: University of Hull Press, 1983.

Kitzman, Laurence. *Auschwitz and After. Race, Culture and "the Jewish Question" in France*. New York: Routledge, 1995.

Koblansky, E. and E. G. Livshits. "A Morphological Approach to the Problem of the Biological Similarity of Jewish and Non-Jewish Populations." *Annals of Human Biology* 12 (1985): 203–12.

Korn, Yitzhak. *Jews at the Crossroads*. New York: Cornwall Books, 1983.

Krogman, Wilton. "The Concept of Race." In Ralph Linton, ed. *The Science of Man in the World Crisis*. New York: Columbia University Press, 1944, 38–62.

Lagmuir, Gavin. *History, Religion, and Antisemitism*. Berkeley: University of California Press, 1990.

———. *Towards a Definition of Antisemitism*. Berkeley: University of California Press, 1990.

Lazare, Bernard. *Antisemitism: Its History and Causes*. London: Briton, 1977.

Leon, H. J. *The Jews of Ancient Rome*. Philadelphia: Jewish Publication Society of America, 1960.

Lerner, Richard. *Final Solutions, Biology, Prejudice, and Genocide*. University Park: Pennsylvania State University Press, 1992.

Leroy-Beaulieu, Anatole. *Israel among the Nations, A Study of Jews and Anti-semitism*. London: G. P. Putnam's Sons, 1896.

Leslie, Donald Daniel. *The Survival of the Chinese Jews: The Jewish Community of Kaifeng*. Leiden, The Netherlands: E. J. Brill, 1972.

Levin, Nora. *The Jews in the Soviet Union since 1917: Paradox of Survival*. New York: New York University Press, 1988.

Lewis, Bernard. *Semites and Anti-Semites. An Inquiry into Conflict and Prejudice*. New York: W. W. Norton & Company, 1986.

Liss, Peggy. *Isabel the Queen: Life and Times*. New York: Oxford University Press, 1992.

Livingstone, Frank. "On the Non-Existence of Human Races." *Current Anthropology* III (1962): 279–81.

Lord, J. Henry. *The Jews in India and the Far East*. Westport, CT: Greenwood Press, 1976.

Lunel, Armand. *Juifs du Languedoc, de Provence, et des états français du pape: Présence du Judaism*. Paris: Albin Michel, 1975.

McClain, Ellen Jaffe. *Embracing the Stranger: Intermarriage and the Future of the American Jewish Community*. New York: Basic Books, 1995.

Malcione, Jose V. *The African Origin of Modern Judaism: From Hebrews to Jews*. Trenton, NJ: Africa World Press, Inc., 1996.

Malino, Frances. *The Sephardic Jews of Bordeaux: Assimilation and Emanci-*

pation in Revolutionary and Napoleonic France. Tuscaloosa: University of Alabama Press, 1978.

Mann, Vivian, B. Thomas, F. Glick, and Jerrilyn D. Dodds. *Convivencia, Jews, Muslims, and Christians in Medieval Spain*. New York: George Braziller and the Jewish Museum, 1992.

Margolis, Max, and Alexander Max. *History of the Jewish People*. New York: Athenum, 1974.

Marrus, Michael. *The Politics of Assimilation: The French Jewish Community at the Time of the Dreyfus Affair*. Oxford: Clarendon Press, 1971.

Mehlman, Jeffrey. *Legacies of Anti-Semitism in France*. Minneapolis: University of Minnesota Press, 1983.

Memmi, Albert. *Portrait d'un juif*. Paris: Gallimard, 1962.

Mendels, Doron. *The Rise and Fall of Jewish Nationalism and Christian Ethnicity in Ancient Palestine*. New York: Anchor Bible Reference Library, Doubleday, 1992.

Montagu, Ashley. *The Concept of Race*. New York: Free Press; London: Collier Macmillan Limited, 1963.

———. *Culture and Evolution of Man*. New York: Oxford University Press, 1962.

———. *Human Heredity*. New York: World Publishing Co., 1959.

———. *Man's Most Dangerous Myth. The Fallacy of Race*, 4th ed. New York: World Publishing, 1964.

Moscati, Sabatino. *Ancient Semitic Civilizations*. New York: G. P. Putman, 1958.

Moss, George. *Towards the Final Solution: A History of European Racism*. Madison: University of Wisconsin Press, 1985.

Moulinas, René. *Les Juifs du pape en France: Les communautés d'Avignon et du Contat Venaissin au 17ème et 18ème siecle*. Paris: Franco Judica, 1981.

Mourant, A. E., Ada C. Kopec, and Kamiera Dominiewska-Sobczak. *The Genetics of the Jews. Research Monographs on Human Population Biology*. Oxford: Clarendon Press, 1978.

Muller-Hill, Benno. *Murderous Science: Elimination by Scientific Selection of Jews, Gypsies, and Others. Germany, 1933–1945*. New York: Oxford University Press, 1988.

Musleah, Ezekiel. *On the Banks of the Ganga. The Sojourn of Jews in Calcutta*. North Quincy, MA: Christopher Publishing House, 1975.

Needle, Patricia. *East Gate of Kaifeng: A Jewish World inside China*. Minneapolis: University of Minnesota Press; China Center, 1992.

Neher, Bernaheim Renee. *Histoire Juive de la Renaissance à nos Jours*. Tomes 1 & 2. Paris: Editions Durlacher, 1963.

Netanyahu, Benzion. *The Marranos of Spain*. New York: American Academy for Jewish Research, Maurice Jacobs Press, 1966.

———. *The Origins of the Inquisition in Fifteenth Century Spain*. New York: Random House, 1995.

Nikiprowetzky, Valentin. *De l'antijudaisme antique à l'antisémitisme contemporain*. Lille: Presses Universitaires de Lille, 1979.

Ochs, Edith, and Bernard Nantet. *Les Falasha, la tribue retrouvée*. Paris: Manya, 1992.

Olender, Maurice. *Le Racisme: Mythes and Sciences*, Brussels: Editions Complexes, 1981.

Oliel, Jacob. *Les Juifs au Sahara: Le Touat au Moyen Age*. Paris: CNRS Editions, 1994.

Parasuran, T. V. *India's Jewish Heritage*. New Delhi: Sagar Publications, 1982.

Paris, Erna. *The End of Days: A Story of Tolerance, Tyranny and the Expulsion of the Jews from Spain*. New York: Prometheus Books, 1995.

Parkes, James. *The Conflict of the Church and the Synagogue*. New York: A Temple Book, Athenum, 1961–1981.

————. *An Enemy of the People: Antisemitism*. New York: Pelican, 1946.

————. *The Jew in the Medieval Community*. London: The Soncino Press, 1930.

————. *The Jewish Problem in the Modern World*. New York: Oxford University Press, 1946.

Perchenet, Annie. *Histoire des Juifs de France*. Paris: Editions du Cerf, 1988.

Perlman, S. M. *The History of the Jews in China*. London: R. Mazin, 1913.

Perry, Mary Elizabeth, and Anne J. Cruz. *Cultural Encounters: The Impact of the Inquisition in Spain and The New World*. Berkeley: University of California Press, 1991.

Peters, Edward. *Inquisition*. Berkeley and Los Angeles: University of California Press, 1989.

Pisar, Samuel. *Of Blood and Hope*. Boston: Little Brown, 1979.

Pitman, G. B. "Judaism: Race or Religion" (1883). *Contemporary Jewish Record* 6 (1943)z; 436–48.

Polednak, Anthony. *Racial and Ethnic Differences in Disease*. New York: Oxford University Press, 1989.

Poliakov, Leon. *The Aryan Myth: A History of Racist and Nationalistic Ideas in Europe*. New York: Basic Books, 1974.

————. *L'Europe suicidaire*. Paris: Calmann-Levy, 1957.

————. *Harvest of Hate, The Nazi Program for the Destruction of the Jews of Europe*. Westport, CT: Greenwood Press, 1979.

————. *The History of Antisemitism*. 4 vols. New York: Vanguard Press, 1965–75.

————. *Hommes et Bêtes*. Paris: Editions Mouton, 1975.

Post, Peter. Anthropological Aspects of Pigmentation, a paper presented at the 43th annual meeting of the American Association of Physical Anthropologist. *American Journal of Physical Anthropology*, 43 (1974): 383–87.

Rabi, A. *Anatomie du judaisme français*. Paris: Editions de Minuit, 1962.

Radin, Max. *The Jewish People. The Jews among the Greeks and Romans*. New York: Arno Press, 1973.

Rajsfus, Maurice. *Jeudi noir*. Paris: Editions de L'Harmattan, 1988.

―――. *Des Juifs dans la colloboration, L'UGIF*. Paris: Etudes et Documenta-
tions Internationales, 1980.

Reinach, Theodore. *Textes d'auteurs Grecs et Romains relatifs au Judaism*.
Reprinted by Greg Olms Verlag Buchhandlung Hildeshein, 1963.

Reinhartz, Jeduha. *Living with Antisemitism: Modern Jewish Responses*.
Waltham, MA: Brandeis University Press, 1987.

Renan, Ernest. *Le judaisme comme race et comme religion*. Paris: Michel
Levis Frères, 1883.

Rice, Michael. *False Inheritance. Israel in Palestine and the Search for a Solution*. London and New York: Kegan Paul International, 1994.

Richarz, Momika. *Jewish Life In Germany: Memoirs of Three Centuries*.
Bloomington: Indiana University Press, 1991.

Riley, Vernon. *Pigmentation: Its Genesis and Biological Control*. New York:
Appleton-Century Crofts, 1972.

Roblin, Michael. *Les Juifs de Paris*. Paris: Picard, 1952.

Roland, Joan G. *Jews in British India*. Waltham, MA: Brandeis University
Press, 1989.

Roth, Cecil. *A Short History of the Jewish People*. London: East and West Library, 1948.

―――. *A History of the Jews in England*. Oxford: Oxford University Press,
1964.

Roth, Norman. *Conversos, Inquisition and the Expulsion of the Jews from
Spain*. Madison: University of Wisconsin Press, 1995.

―――. *Jews Visigoths, and Muslims in Miedeval Spain*. New York: E. J. Brill,
1994.

Roudinesco, Alexandre. *Le malheur d'Israel*. Paris: Editions Cluny, 1956.

Rousso, Henry. *The Vichy Syndrome*. Cambridge, MA: Harvard University
Press, 1991.

Ruether, Rosemary Radford. *Faith and Fraticide. The Theological Roots of
Antisemitism*. New York: Seabury Press, 1974.

Ruppin, Arthur. *The Jews of Today*. New York: Henry Holt.

Sachar, Abram Leon. *A History of the Jews*. New York: Alfred Knopf, 1966.

Sachar, Howard. *Farewell Espania. The World of the Sephardim Remembered*. New York: Alfred A. Knopf, 1994.

Samuel, Shellim. *A Treatise of the Origins and Early History of the Beni-Israel
of the Maharashtra State*. Bombay: Iyer and Iyer, 1963.

Sartre, Jean-Paul. *Relexions sur la question juive*. Paris: Paul Morihien, 1946.

Schafer, Peter. *Judeophobia. Attitudes towards the Jews in the Ancient World*.
Cambridge, MA: Harvard University Press, 1997.

Schurer, Emil. *A History of the Jewish People in the Time of Jesus Christ*. New
York: Charles Scribner, n.d.

Schwarzfuchs, Simon. *Du juif a l'israelite: Histoire d'une mutation*. Paris: Fayard, 1989.

―――. *Les Juifs de France*. Paris: Albin Michel, 1975.

Segal, J. B. *History of the Jews of Cochin*. London: Valentine Mitchell, 1993.

Selznick, Gertrude, and Stephen Steinberg. *The Tenacity of Prejudice.* New York: Harper and Row, 1969.

Sern, Menahuen. *Greek and Latin Authors on Jews and Judaism.* Jerusalem: Israel Academy of Science and Humanities, 1984.

Sevenster, J. N. *The Roots of Pagan Anti-Semitism in the Ancient World.* Leiden, The Netherlands: E. J. Brill, 1975.

Shapiro, Harry. *The Jewish People: A Biological History. The Race Question in Modern Science.* New York: Columbia University Press, 1961.

Shapiro, Sidney. *Jews in Old China.* New York: Hypocrene Books, 1984.

Sherwin-White, A. N. *Racial Prejudice in Imperial Rome.* Cambridge: Cambridge University Press, 1967.

Shipman, Pat. *The Evolution of Racism: Human Differences and the Use and Abuse of Science.* New York: Simon and Schuster, 1994.

Simmel, Ernst. *Anti-Semitism. A Social Disease.* New York: International Universities Presses, 1946.

Simon, Marcel. *Verus Israel.* New York: Oxford University Press, 1986.

Steinman, Lionel. *Paths to Genocide. Antisemitism in Western History.* New York: St. Martin Press, 1988.

Strizower, Schiffra. *The Children of Israel: The Bene Israel of Bombay.* Oxford: Basil Blackwell, 1971.

———. *Exotic Jewish Communities.* London: Thomas Yoseloff, 1962.

Vidal-Naquet, Pierre. *The Jews: History, Memory and the Present.* New York: Columbia University Press, 1996.

Vishniak, Mark. *An International Convention against Antisemitism.* New York: Research Institute of the Jewish Labor Committee, 1946.

Washburn, Sherwood. "The Study of Race." *American Anthropologist* 16 (1963): 521–53.

Weinberg, David. *A Community in Trial. The Jews of Paris in the 1930s.* Chicago: University of Chicago Press, 1977.

Weinberg, Meyer. *Because They Were Jews, A History of Antisemitism.* New York: Greenwood Press, 1986.

Wise, Ruth R. *If I am not Myself.* New York: Free Press, 1990.

Wistrich, Robert. *Antisemitism. The Longest Hatred.* London: Thames Methuen, 1995.

Wyman, David. *Abandonment of the Jews, America and the Holocaust (1941–1945).* New York: Pantheon Books, 1984.

Zolchan, I. *Are the Jews a Race?* Vienna: Braumeller, 1912.

Zuccoti, Susan. *The Holocaust, the French, and the Jews.* New York: Basic Books, 1993.

Index